# On the Miss Middleton Effect

Geraldine E. Rodgers

authorHOUSE

*AuthorHouse™*
*1663 Liberty Drive*
*Bloomington, IN 47403*
*www.authorhouse.com*
*Phone: 833-262-8899*

*Published by AuthorHouse 07/20/2022*

*ISBN: 978-1-6655-6555-4 (sc)*
*ISBN: 978-1-6655-6556-1 (e)*

*Print information available on the last page.*

*Any people depicted in stock imagery provided by Getty Images are models, and such images are being used for illustrative purposes only.*
*Certain stock imagery © Getty Images.*

*This book is printed on acid-free paper.*

# Contents

# CHAPTER 1

# The Background on "Silent Reading Comprehension" Tests

It was over a hundred years ago that Miss Middleton's silent reading comprehension scores and others like them were recorded by the Sycamore, Illinois, Superintendent of Schools Karl Douglas Waldo. Those scores now provide the necessary proof to indict the "reading experts" of his day and of our day for almost destroying America's freely functioning literacy.

Yet those 1913-1914 scores may very well have cost Waldo his job as Superintendent of Schools in Sycamore, Illinois. By January of the very next year, 1915, when Waldo reported his 1913-1914 results in the Elementary School Journal, he was shown instead as Principal of East Aurora High School, Aurora, Illinois.

Waldo's 1913-1914 scores concerned so-called "silent reading comprehension," which, as will be shown, was unheard of before 1870. Most primary school teachers today would see nothing really wrong with the "silent reading comprehension" lessons or the "silent reading comprehension" tests that took over American schools after the arrival of the reading texts in 1930 that were using a deaf-mute method to teach reading. That circa 1930 take-over happened only sixteen years after Waldo published his 1913-1914 scores. (Of course, those primary school teachers have no idea that they, themselves, are teaching with what is an inferior deaf-mute method whenever they promote context-guessing in reading.)

Silent reading comprehension lessons and silent reading comprehension tests were the obvious outgrowths of the deaf-mute, "sentence", "meaning" reading method that began to be promoted in 1870, over 40 years before Waldo's tests. No one ever comments on the fact that such silent lessons and silent tests for children with normal hearing were apparently unknown before the 1870 arrival of the sentence version of the deaf-mute method, except in a book, The Mother's Primer, for both hearing and deaf children. That had been published in 1835 by the famous teacher of deaf children, Thomas Hopkins Gallaudet, but it was apparently not very widely used. However, Gallaudet did not use the sentence method, so that version was new in 1870.

In a speech to the 1873 National Education Association, George L. Farnham reported on his use of what he called the sentence method, which method he later discussed in his 1881 book, The

Sentence Method of Teaching Reading. His book was published by C. W. Bardeen of Syracuse, New York, who also published the excellent School Bulletin from 1874 to 1920.

In 1870, Farnham had experimented with the sentence method in the schools of Binghamton, New York. A first-grade teacher was to write a whole sentence on the blackboard in front of beginners who could not yet read at all. The teacher was to use silent motions and various articles to enable the children to guess the meaning of the whole written sentence.

The rationale for the use of the sentence method was the belief that sentences are totally unbreakable in their meaning and should therefore always be presented to children initially as "wholes", and only later be broken into their written parts. Yet Farnham did not claim to have originated the idea that reading should always be taught in whole sentences because whole sentences, not isolated words, are the real meaning-bearing units in language.

Twenty years after Farnham's 1870 experiment, in William James' 1890 The Principles of Psychology, and with no reference to Farnham, James made it clear that he thought that he was the originator of the idea that the sentence is the totally unbreakable and primary unit in thought. Strangely, at the level of the unconscious mind, not the conscious mind, in what the neurologist/ surgeon Dr. Wilder Penfield named the automatic sensory-motor mechanism, there is some evidence that syntax, as in a sentence, does automatically control the choice of words and therefore must be the primary unit. For the automatic control of words of grammar in a sentence, see page 22, Two Sides of the Brain, Brain Lateralization Explained, Sid J. Segalowitz, Prentice-Hall, Inc., Englewood Cliffs, New Jersey, 1983. It appears that James may have been right about the sentence being the unbreakable unit in thought, but that would manifestly be only at the unconscious level, not the conscious level which was being used by Farnham.

It is interesting that William James was commissioned in 1878 by the Holt publishers to write his book on psychology, but it did not come out until 1890, many, many years later. James contracted to write his book on psychology some years after he began to teach at Harvard in 1872. That was a year before the sentence method became public with the publishing of Farnham's 1873 book. However, James was apparently unemployed in 1870 when Farnham gave his lesson on the sentence method in Binghamton.

This author's 1998 book, The Hidden Story, discusses the background on Farnham and James in depth. Since Farnham did NOT claim to have invented the idea that the sentence is the primary unit, Farnham apparently somehow became the agent of the famous and first-in-America psychologist, William James, who did publicly claim, 20 years later, to have invented the idea.

One of the very first "silent reading comprehension" tests was written and reported in the 1914 Teachers College Record, Columbia University, New York, by the psychologist, E. L. Thorndike, who had been William James' former student and close friend. In the 1890's, Thorndike had even been permitted to keep his experimental chickens in the basement of William James' home, while Thorndike was doing graduate work at Harvard under William James. Although others in Thorndike's circle also began working on "silent reading comprehension" tests in 1913-1914, perhaps it was Thorndike's model which won out. The "silent reading comprehension" tests today are only variations of what Thorndike originally prepared.

As discussed, in that same 1914 article in which Thorndike reported on his "silent reading comprehension test," he reported on the oral reading accuracy test of his graduate student, William Scott Gray. It was Gray, 16 years later, who became the author of the first complete deaf-mute method reading series, the famous 1930 "Dick and Jane" readers published by Scott, Foresman, which did away with the use of any isolated "sound" in the teaching of reading. After 1930, for almost 40 years, that "Dick and Jane" series inundated the United States, from Coast to Coast.

The two original deaf-mute method readers, the 1930 series published by Scott, Foresman and the 1931 series published by Macmillan, were written by the two most prominent "reading experts" of that time, and both had been Thorndike's students. William Scott Gray of the University of Chicago was the principal author of the 1930 Scott, Foresman "Dick and Jane" series (which was used in revised forms until the late 1960's). Arthur Irving Gates of Columbia Teachers College was the principal author of the 1931 Macmillan series (later replaced as principal author by Albert J. Harris). Gray and Gates were the "academic" sons of Thorndike, and therefore the "academic" grandsons of William James.

Thorndike's 1913-1914 "silent reading comprehension tests" were later refined in concert with his co-author and graduate student, William A. McCall, who received his doctorate from Columbia in 1916 on those tests. McCall's thesis was published in 1916 by Columbia Teachers College and reported in the Teachers College Record in articles in 1915 and 1916 as "An Improved Scale for Measuring Ability in Reading." The material was acknowledged to be the forerunner of the Thorndike-McCall Reading Tests (TCR, page 494, February, 1926).

Some of McCall's reading tests in their later versions, which are revisions of the "Thorndike-McCall" material, may still be in use. They have the same format as the "silent reading comprehension" tests in use today: paragraphs of whole sentences followed by questions on content. But the later McCall material, like the SRA cards that once were so common in classrooms, were supposed to be "test-lessons," and not just tests. They not only "tested" silent reading comprehension but were supposed, for some reason this writer has never understood, also to TEACH silent reading comprehension. A series of test cards were provided which the child took in sequence and which he marked himself. (Such a program did encourage attention: If children did not want to score so badly on subsequent material as they did on the first material, they were likely to pay closer attention to what they were reading on that subsequent material.)

No one ever comments on the historical fact that "silent reading comprehension" tests for people with normal hearing were totally unknown, ALL THROUGH HUMAN HISTORY, until the advent of the first experimental psychologists such as William James, James McKeen Cattell and Edward L. Thorndike. Although psychologists began promoting such tests seriously only in 1913-1914, the rationale supporting such testing certainly predated 1913-1914 and certainly went back as far as to Farnham in 1870.

The rationale certainly went back as far as to that very first sentence silently written on the blackboard in front of those Binghamton, New York, children who could not yet read. The children were being prompted to guess the meaning of that whole sentence solely from the motions of the teacher and from the objects held by the teacher. That sentence on that Binghamton blackboard in 1870 was the very first "silent reading comprehension" test, and it was written for children who could not yet read a single word.


## Is Reading Comprehension a Teachable Skill?

In discussing so-called "reading comprehension" and whether or not it is a teachable skill that can be tested, it will be necessary to include a considerable amount of historical background information. Much is generally unknown but is needed at this point to understand the topic more fully.

Is so-called "reading comprehension" actually a "skill" that can be taught? "Teachable" means "conditionable". Learning ("conditioning") is stored in the part of the brain that the famous neurologist/surgeon Dr. Wilder Penfield named the "sensory-motor mechanism". (Dr. Penfield discussed this in his text, The Mystery of the Mind, Princeton University Press, Princeton, New Jersey, 1975.) The sensory-motor mechanism seems to be like an inborn, totally unconscious computer. The sensory-motor mechanism is involved whenever a conditioned "skill" is stored or is called for later by what Dr Penfield called "the higher brain mechanism," which is the conscious part of the brain. The "skill" might be the skill of reading correctly and automatically, or the skill of playing the piano correctly and automatically, or the skill of riding a bike, or the remembering of dates in history or telephone numbers, and on and on.

Dr. Hilde Mosse worked for years in the New York City schools, and eventually wrote her superb two-volume work, The Complete Handbook of Children's Reading Disorders, Human Sciences Press, Inc., New York, 1982. On page 28 of Volume I, she wrote:

> "Reading Disorders can be caused by an inability to form the necessary conditioned reflexes, or by the establishment and practice of wrong reflexes."

In her work, Dr. Mosse referred to some comments made by Dr. Wilder Penfield, to the effect that we can learn ("condition") only those things on which we focus conscious attention at the time they are being learned.

Put both these learned statements together, that of Dr. Mosse and Dr. Penfield: It is reasonable to assume that someone without a reading disorder has formed the correct reading reflexes, per Dr. Mosse. Yet is also reasonable to assume that someone, despite having the correct reading reflexes, would not learn anything from material he read unless he focused his conscious attention on it, per Dr. Penfield. That two-part statement will explain the results from Miss Middleton's class, to be discussed later.

A definite point was made in my book, The Critical Missed Step. It is that the organic path that is automatically followed in the brain for listening to oral speech, from syllables to syntax and finally to conscious meaning, is the same organic path that should be automatically followed for printed speech. That is what reading matter really is, printed speech. For both oral speech and printed speech, the first two steps, syllables to syntax, (the learned and stored skill steps) should be done automatically. That third and last step, meaning, (not a stored skill step) is obviously and necessarily a conscious step. However, if consciousness is used on either of the first two automatic steps, or if any of those three steps (syllables to syntax to meaning) are omitted, that demonstrates the presence of a disability in hearing or in reading.

The basic problem with the deaf-mute, context-guessing method for reading is that it interferes with what should be the normal path for listening to speech, both oral and written. The normal path is (1) syllables to (2) syntax (with both steps automatic) and then (3) consciousness, which, by definition, cannot be automatic. However, the deaf-mute method makes the second step, syntax, a conscious step because it uses context-guessing. Then, as might be expected for a method invented for the deaf, it completely removes the first step, syllables. That leaves only one level: conscious guessing. Therefore, by definition, the deaf-mute method is not automatic as it has removed the automatic steps. All that is left is consciousness.

Classes that can read automatically by the use of learned decoding skills can produce typical "skill graphs" for these skills if the teaching has been successful, with scores piling up towards the end, the "almost everybody succeeds" end. But, the context-guessing deaf-mute method to read is not automatic and so is not a skill. It relies on conscious guessing. A graph for deaf-mute method reading scores will be more like a spread-out bell graph, the kind of graph that reflects inborn qualities like the intelligence used to guess.

In contrast to whole-class "skill" teaching where all children are taught at the same time and most succeed, ability grouping in classrooms began to be promoted after the arrival of the deaf mute method. Ability grouping of students became mandatory with the deaf-mute "meaning" method because conscious intelligence is needed for guessing. Therefore, a class of like-aged children could no longer succeed as a single group but fell into sharply different groups: bright, average, and slow. The hour and a half in a school day that a teacher once had available to teach reading to the whole class turned into three 30-minute periods for each group in the class. The new method deprived each student of one hour each day of the teacher's personal attention.

First-grade classes were apparently not "ability-grouped" for reading instruction in the 1920's, except probably in the "experts'" experimental schools. It was in 1930 and 1931 that the deaf-mute, sight-word, context-guessing "meaning" method in reading instruction finally arrived in American schools, but it did require ability grouping because it was drawing on the innate intelligence of the children to "guess". The complete deaf-mute method used sight-words and context-guessing. It used jig-saw puzzle phonics. Jig-saw puzzle phonics is the pulling off of parts from remembered sight words to match a new, unknown word, and has nothing to do with real sound. This context-guessing approach was called "intrinsic phonics" and appeared in the new, post-1930, reading series, eventually through sixth grade.

In the fall of 1977, when this author's European oral reading accuracy research was done, most European schools tested used whole class instruction, not group instruction. All European second grade classes scored very high in oral reading accuracy. This is just what might have been expected. The conditioned reflexes underlying correct oral reading production are skills, and properly-taught skills in any normal group produce a typically shaped graph. They pile up towards the very highest end of the graph scale. When skills are taught properly, almost ALL of a normal group can be expected to succeed, and so there is no "need" to group for ability.

By contrast, a bell-shaped graph curve is highest in the middle, and then slides down to almost nothing at either end (very high or very low). Reportedly, true bell-shaped graph curves are only produced if they involve INNATE or inborn qualities in any normal population, such as IQ (intelligence quotient) scores or even women's shoe sizes. Such qualities are not teachable, unlike skills, which are teachable. But it is only an inborn ability (intelligence), not skill, that is being called on in deaf-mute-method reading comprehension. Since all of the method's reading comprehension activity is conscious, and since nothing else is used that could qualify as a skill, then its reading comprehension activity is not teachable.

Is Conscious Attention Free or Controlled?

As stated previously, the organic path that is automatically followed in the brain for listening to oral speech, from syllables to syntax and finally to conscious meaning, is the same organic path that should be automatically followed for printed speech. For both oral speech and printed speech, the first two steps, syllables to syntax, (the learned and stored skill steps) should be done automatically. That third and last step, meaning, (not a stored skill step) is obviously and necessarily a conscious step.

However, there is a further and a very contentious step, indeed, and it concerns the last level, the conscious level. Is human consciousness free or not free in choosing its objects of conscious attention (such as vanilla or chocolate, or whether or not to pay attention to a boring speaker) or are such choices of focusing the attention at the conscious level controlled in some way? Is there really a free choice? Can attention be voluntary? Can it freely be turned on and off, and then back on again?

It is therefore not surprising that it is the contentious question "Can attention be voluntary?" that has been at the very foundation of the reading instruction wars ever since the early nineteenth century. The question concerns whether or not consciousness can freely choose where to focus its attention. The first two automatic steps in reading printed language, syllables to syntax, might be successful, and so might the third step, reaching consciousness of meaning. Yet, at that third step, once reached, is that consciousness actually forced to listen to the meaning of the printed language stream that is being automatically produced for it by its brain's computer? Or can that consciousness choose to turn away from that printed language stream that is being automatically produced, just as it can turn away from a spoken language stream that is being automatically produced from a boring lecturer? Once turned off, can it be turned back on again, at will?

The boring lecturer may continue to speak, and the listener's ears will still be hearing him, automatically, but the listener's free attention may have turned him off. So it should also certainly be possible for a person to continue to read automatically, but with his free attention to the reading turned off. That kind of mindless automatic reading can probably be done orally by someone in front of an audience, at the same time that the conscious, free attention of that someone may be on worrying about whether or not he is going to have enough time left to catch a bus. That someone can, in a split second, turn his attention back from the bus to what he is reading aloud.

Probably, the question, "Can attention be voluntary?" is never directly raised in connection with reading, but only implicitly. So far as I know, it has never been openly discussed in connection with reading. Perhaps that is because the question of free attention does involve religion, which fact was made very clear by no one less than the philosopher/psychologist, William James, as will be shown.

Yet, as will also be shown, the early "reading experts" threw that kind of "automaticity" in reading out the window. The "experts'" method got rid of the ability to read automatically, which means to continue to read even when the conscious mind chooses to wander to something else. The "experts" succeeded in replacing that automaticity in reading with the use of the conscious mind plus context guessing to decode print. The no-longer-reading-automatically readers now had to guess their way down any page, in the same basic way as those 1870 Binghamton beginners.


## What Has Resulted

It is absolutely shocking to learn, from a 1980 United States Government study, how well the "experts" ever since 1914 have succeeded in damaging what is probably almost all of our American population. The following appears on page 11 of <u>Becoming a, Nation of Readers, The Report of the Commission on Reading</u>, The National Institute of Education, U. S. Department of Education, Washington, D. C., 1985:

"The generally accepted current model of word identification [is that] a possible interpretation of a word usually begins forming in the mind as soon as even partial information has been gleaned about the letters in the word... When enough evidence from the letters and the context becomes available, the possible interpretation becomes a positive identification."

This model, using context and conscious guessing for word identification, which was based on actual tests on living American readers, implies that automaticity is lacking for these readers, not just on unfamiliar words, but on almost ALL words! This awful statement confirms that the American readers they tested can only read print by the use of conscious guessing, just like partially deaf people who are trying to follow a conversation, and just like those 1870 Binghamton beginners. The readers have to guess their way consciously down a page.

So the "experts", both past and present, have unfortunately won, and they are still very firmly in the driver's seat, continuing to turn out new generations of disabled American readers, who are forced to read print consciously, not automatically.

## Concerning Automaticity in Reading

Concerning the differences between the two types of reading, "psycholinguistically" guessing or automatic skill reading, some unrelated research does have a connection with those topics.

Mentioned in my book, The Critical Missed Step, was the case described by Dr. R. M. N. Crosby, in his text, The Waysiders, Delacorte Press, New York, 1968, page 103, about a British physician in the early nineteenth century, Dr. Lordot. In 1843, Dr. Lordot told of his temporary loss of ability to read in 1825. Before that date, the use of complete syllable tables for beginners had been the norm. Dr. Lordat, who was fully grown in 1825, would have almost certainly learned to read by the syllable tables, just as a baby learning to speak babbles syllable sounds Lordat reported in 1843:

"Whilst retaining the significance of words heard, I had lost that of their visible signs. Syntax had disappeared along with words: the alphabet alone was left to me, but the function of the letter for the formation of words was a study yet to be made.... After several weeks of profound badness and resignation, I discovered whilst looking from a distance at the back of one of the volumes in my library that I was reading accurately the title Hippocratis Opera."

Dr. Lordat's temporary loss of ability to read had been total, except for the letters of the alphabet, which are thought to be stored on the right side of the brain, where the Japanese Kanji meaning-bearing characters are known to be stored. Therefore, Dr. Lordat's stroke must not have been on the right side of the brain but on the left side of the brain. Dr. Lordat must have learned to read some considerable time before 1825, when reading was taught by the sound-bearing syllabary. The syllabary, which is pure sound, would have been stored on the left or language side of Dr. Lordot's brain. That is where the Japanese Kana syllables are known to be stored, and so would Dr. Lordat's spelling book words which later were built from that sound-bearing syllable foundation. He therefore needed syllable sounds in reading, just as in listening. As a result, Dr. Lordat could not read any words at all when the left, sound side of his brain for reading was blocked by a stroke.

Also discussed in <u>The Critical Missed Step</u> was a <u>New York Times</u> article of May 2, 1985, by Daniel Goleman, entitled "Insights Into Self Deception" In carrying out their research, a group had devised a lens so that words could be read by the right hemisphere of the brain alone or by the left hemisphere of the brain alone. Obviously, Dr. Lordat could not have been one of their subjects, as he could only handle left-brain print, but these researchers were drawing on a 20<sup>th</sup> century population which had initially been taught to read some meaning-bearing words, as well as some phonics on words, and so had some use of both left and right.

The research group of Davidson/Perl/Saron reported on a time lag in the response to images of emotionally disturbing, negative words if the words were projected to be read by the right hemisphere, but there was no such time lag if the words were projected to be read by the left hemisphere. Therefore, with the right hemisphere, the meaning of words was perceived before the words were spoken. So reading on the right does result in consciousness of the meaning of each individual word before it is spoken. However, when using the left hemisphere, the words were spoken automatically before the meaning was perceived. That means that reading on the left is done automatically, without the use of consciousness.

Dr. Lordat, a syllable-trained reader, could only use his left side to read. Since reading on that side is automatic, without the use of consciousness, that meant that Dr, Lordat was an automatic reader and was incapable (lucky him!) of reading psycholinguistically. He was reading completely automatically.

Dr. Lordat's case supports the argument for the existence of automatic reading, or "skill" reading, as opposed to the deaf-mute method, which goes down a page by conscious, psycholinguistic guessing.

The use of the terms, "psycholinguistic guessing" may be a lot older than is generally realized in America because I saw the term, "psycholinguistique", in a 1951 article in <u>Enfance</u>, Paris, France. A previous <u>Enfance</u> article had been mentioned in another publication I saw so I had looked for and found the previous article. It was a January-February 1950 <u>Enfance</u> article on research entitled <u>Etude de Quarante Cas de Dyslexie d'Evolution</u>, by Mme. Roudinesco, Jean Trelat and Mme. Trelat. On page 7 of the article, the following statement was made:

> "We point out, however, that in the schools with the analytic [Editor: sound] method we could find only 2% dyslexics, whereas 20% of the children have these typical troubles in the new schools where the global [Editor: meaning] method only was employed."

That 1950 article brought on a waterfall of what appeared to be pro-meaning and anti-sound articles in a 1951 issue of <u>Enfance</u>. It was in one of those that I saw the word, "psycholinguistique." The article was by Suzanne Borel-Maisonny and was entitled "Les Troubles de Langage dans les Dyslexies et les Dysorthographies."

The Russian psychologist, D. B. Elkonin, Institute of Psychology, Academy of Educational Science, once gave his own definition of reading.

> "In the present paper, we start from the proposition that reading is a reconstitution of the sound forms of a word on the basis of its graphic representation. Understanding, which is often considered as the basic content of the process of reading arises as a result of correct recreation of the sound forms of words. He who, independently of

the level of understanding of words, can correctly recreate their sound forms is able to read." (Page 165, Brian and Joan Simon, <u>Educational Psychology in the U.S.S.R,</u>, Stanford University Press, Stanford, California, 1963)

Elkonin's definition was the opposite of the definition that might have been expected from the American psychologist, E. L. Thorndike. Elkonin's definition implied that reading should be automatic, in the sense of simply turning print into speech. His definition for reading had appeared in his article, "The Psychology of Mastering the Elements of Reading". It should be remembered that the Soviet Union reported no illiteracy problem. Elkonin certainly would not have fitted in with the 1911 and later "experts" in the United States.

# CHAPTER 2

# The Research Results
# from Superintendent Waldo
# and Miss Middleton

A window into what was the new and exploding "reading expert" world of 1911 and later can be found in William Scott Gray's 1917 doctoral degree thesis at the University of Chicago. Gray's bibliography lists most of the known "reading research" up to that date, with authors' names and topics. Gray listed Karl D. Waldo's 1915 thesis, which has already been mentioned.

In the January, 1915, <u>Elementary School Journal</u> of the University of Chicago, Waldo had reported that the elementary school he tested in 1913 and 1914 had used the famous Ward Rational System of Reading (heavy phonics) in first and second grades since 1909. For a small group in the recent past, another heavily phonic program by W. W. Howe had been used. Therefore, Waldo's third and fourth grade children had definitely been taught to read by phonic "sound," not by sight word "meaning."

Waldo's thesis at a school like the University of Chicago, in a year like 1913-1914, was, not surprisingly, on reading instruction. It reported on the testing he had done of all eight grades in a Sycamore elementary school, including Miss Middleton's class. The record suggests that, when Waldo's thesis clearly demonstrated that his students were reading automatically because the "silent reading comprehension" scores were wildly random, it may have cost him his position. At that time, no one knew how to evaluate the brand-new so-called "silent reading comprehension" scores that were producing such bizarre results. No one had raised the question of whether or not there could be a critical effect on the scores from the presence or absence of voluntary attention.

At this point, it is well to introduce Miss Middleton's class of 1913 and 1914 and her individual testing scores, which will be discussed. They provide virtual proof that, unlike today's students as shown by the 1980 Government study, Miss Middleton's students in 1913 and 1914 were automatic readers. However, in the "expert"-plagued atmosphere of that time, her scores were undoubtedly misunderstood. Also, it is appropriate to discuss Karl Douglas Waldo, who had obviously been a responsible and successful Superintendent of Schools in Sycamore, Illinois, for years, since he had served there from 1909 through 1914, and he also had been studying for an advanced degree at the University of Chicago.

That subset from Waldo's whole-school research results, the Miss Middleton results, listed children's individual scores in both September and March. Her third and fourth grade children had been taught to read by "sound." When comparing each child's September score to his or her March score, a wild difference usually appeared. That very clearly raised the question of the presence or absence of voluntary attention. Yet Waldo apparently never commented on that seemingly obvious fact, that the scores were almost totally random. That is certainly curious.

In some past material, I had referred to Miss Middleton's interesting individual scores from Waldo's thesis, but I can no longer locate the source. It might be on my computer disk labeled "Waldo", which I can no longer open. Therefore, I downloaded from the Internet Waldo's entire January, 1915, article in the Elementary School Journal of the University of Chicago, reporting on his thesis, and it included that interesting individual data on Miss Middleton's class.

Waldo probably did that work under the psychologist, Charles Hubbard Judd, who had been the fellow student of E. L. Thorndike at Wesleyan, and under whom William Scott Gray, the ex-student of Thorndike, was working at the University of Chicago by 1917. That would have put Waldo right in the middle of the top group of "experts".

Waldo reported that each of the eight grades had been given appropriate reading material to read silently for five minutes. The children were then to indicate where they had stopped in the material at the end of the five minutes. After that, they were to write an account of what they had read, and were given a reasonable amount of time to produce the written account. Finally, they had to answer ten questions on the reading matter, or less than ten questions if they had not finished the reading matter. Obviously, by today's labeling, those ten questions (or sometimes less) were a "silent reading comprehension" test. However, Miss Middleton's class was the only one that reported individual children's scores, as well as class averages.

All grades had been given completely new experiences, and they were probably, for the most part, exciting and stimulating. The probability is that the grades had never before been asked to write out an account of something they had just read. That part they must have found exhausting. It was only after the long, silent five-minute reading period that they had to produce those difficult written summaries. It must have taken an appreciable time for the children to complete those first activities, the five-minute silent reading and the long, written-out account of what they had read. Also, the passing out of materials and the collecting of materials must have taken additional time.

Waldo reported on page 253 of his article in The Elementary School Journal, "Each test took about an hour of school time." Therefore, it was perhaps 40 minutes or more after starting that the children were finally told to answer specific reading comprehension questions on material they had finished reading perhaps 30 minutes or more previously. They were having entertaining days, with different classroom activities instead of the usual routine, but at this point they were to answer specific written questions on material they had read perhaps 30 minutes or more previously, and on which they probably had paid little attention.

When Waldo printed out the final scores from his research, at all grades through the eighth, he got exactly the kind of scores he should have expected from all the grades. He had not been testing anything that had actually been taught, or testing any real "conditionable" skills. He had only been testing the degree of attention given to something that had been of no importance to the takers of the test, and it had been done on days in which the test-takers would have been excited because of the new activities.

Furthermore, since probably most of the children at all grades, including fifth to eighth had been taught to read by phonic "sound," and not sight-word "meaning," they could read automatically and had no need for conscious guessing. They had completely free attention, to focus or not to focus on what they were reading. Obviously, on those unusual days, they did not feel like focusing that free attention. Therefore, it is not at all surprising that Waldo's reading comprehension scores for the whole school were absolutely horrible.

Presumably, these reading comprehension questions, at all grade levels, were expected to have produced normal passing scores of 70 per cent to 100 per cent. Instead, almost all of these scores for all eight grades were very badly failing scores. That must have been a shattering discovery for unfortunate Superintendent Waldo, who had done nothing wrong.

Of course, Waldo did not report his scores as catastrophic, but produced tables analysing the scores in a positive manner, suggesting improvement in scores from fall to spring. However, appalling scores like Waldo's finally made it possible for the "experts" to promote the deaf-mute "sentence" reading method, even though it was only available at that time in modified versions like the Aldine readers. However, its enlarged use was at the expense of the heavily "sound" based first-grade materials like Wards, which had developed accurate, automatic readers like Waldo's students. In 1913 and 1914, such "sound-based" first-grade materials were in wide use.

Superintendent of Schools Waldo must not have been the only superintendent receiving a jarring experience concerning reading instruction. Superintendents of schools all over America must have been exposed to similar criticism but must not have had any idea of what was really going on. Appalling scores, just like Waldo's, must have been coming in for those superintendents, as soon as they installed the "experts" silent reading comprehension tests. The superintendents did not know that they were not getting real "comprehension" scores. Instead, what they were getting from their phonically taught, and so automatically-reading, children were massive demonstrations of the power of voluntary attention. They did not know that phonics classes who are led to "pay attention" score the highest, as I showed in my text, <u>Why Jacques, Johann and Jan Can Read</u>.

All the wonderful, "expert" advice they were getting from the reading "experts" never suggested that the cause for the "problem" could be anything as simple as the power of voluntary attention.

Like Waldo's students, most students in America at that time had been taught to read by phonic "sound," so their attention was free when reading, to concentrate or to wander. However, those children who were taught by sight-word "meaning" had their attention forced on the "meaning" or they could not read at all. Instead of producing attention-wandering low scores on silent reading comprehension tests, such students could produce consistent and higher scores. Those results made a powerful argument for the reading "experts" to use, and probably explain the Coast-to-Coast adoption of the deaf-mute method after 1930.

Even though the deaf-mute method readers must have produced wonderful silent reading comprehension scores, there is no available record on those circa 1930 students ever having been tested on oral reading accuracy. In 1915, Waldo mentioned oral reading testing twice in his article on his thesis, but the testing of oral reading accuracy was dead and gone well before the adoption of the total deaf-mute method in 1930. After 1930, almost no one knew how badly most of the children were actually reading, outside of their "controlled vocabulary" textbooks.. The children were now like one of my former second grade students, an "A" student, who could read already-learned sight words like chrysanthemum. He asked me to read a hard word that he could not. That "hard" word was something like "frog" (and I do think it was "frog"). Yet most of my first graders, who would have started learning to read in September, could have read that "hard" word before Halloween at the end of October.

It is disturbing fact that no valid, group, oral reading accuracy test results in America have been available ever since William Scott Gray published his 1917 doctoral thesis. That reported on Gray's circa 1916 valid oral reading accuracy testing of grade school classes. Apparently, not long after that, Gray changed his method of scoring so that his test then had very little meaning. However, the Gray test with its faulty methods of scoring was in use for many years, but it was used for individual testing, not class testing. It is probably still in use

The Gilmore Oral Reading Test (1951) and Revised Gilmore Oral Reading Test (1968) are valid tests only for children who were taught to read in the controlled vocabulary deaf-mute method readers, because Gilmore reportedly limited his test vocabulary to the high frequency words found in Thorndike's 10,000 commonest words.

The United States Office of Education (USOE) tests in 1968, at second grade level, seemed to promise some worthwhile oral reading accuracy test results, even though they were using the Gilmore tests.. Yet, as reported in my book, The Critical Missed Step, someone accidentally wiped out those oral reading accuracy results before they could be published. Those 1968 results would have been the only valid group testing results, except fo Gilmore's norms, since Gray's circa 1916 results.

Also as reported in The Critical Missed Step, the so-called oral reading accuracy tests of NAEP (National Assessment of Educational Progress) in 1992 and 2002 were useless, but, even so, what results they did have were disturbingly low.

The NAEP fourth-grade students had been pre-tested and an unknown number of poor readers had been removed from the sample group. Furthermore, the oral reading accuracy test that was used for scoring for those remaining in the sample group had already been read once by those students in silent reading comprehension tests, so it was not new, unpracticed material. After having already had that one chance to practice reading the material, the students then had a second chance (and sometimes more) to read the identical material again silently. The students were finally asked to read the well-practiced material aloud and were scored for accuracy. A group oral reading accuracy test score based on that kind of oral reading accuracy testing by a pre-picked group is obviously meaningless.

So, effectively, the oral reading accuracy of groups of American students has never been tested reliably. Yet we have had massive testing of "silent reading comprehension," even though such tests reveal nothing about reading accuracy, and are actually just tests of intelligence. The first reading comprehension testing was apparently done by the psychologist, Alfred Binet, of France, about 1908, but he used it to evaluate intelligence, not reading accuracy.

There is seemingly no mention in the records that exist today about earlier oral reading accuracy testing, before the arrival of the deaf-mute readers in 1930. However, Waldo's article is very helpful on that point, although almost casually. In his January, 1915, article in the Elementary School Journal, he mentioned on page 251 his own testing and recording of oral reading accuracy, in his position as a school administrator. Then, on page 253, concerning children writing summaries of what they had read, he wrote, "Such a test measures both elements of the reading much better than could be done by listening to the oral reading of the children, as is usually done in supervision".

Apparently, the formal testing of the oral reading accuracy of students had ceased before about 1920. In the 22 years that I taught grades one, two and three, from 1963 to 1985, no one ever checked the oral reading accuracy of the children in my classroom. Instead, their reading was tested by printed "silent reading comprehension" tests and by printed tests on vocabulary meaning.

The children in Waldo's research had not been tested on material which they had been taught, and which they would have felt responsible to remember (as, Columbus and 1492, or 1776 and the Declaration of Independence). They had experienced two very unusual days, one in September and one in March. The children had focused little conscious attention on what it was that they were supposed to read during those days. It is obvious that the contentious question, "Can attention be voluntary?" should definitely be raised at this point.

However, as has been reported, what was very unusual about Waldo's scores for Miss Middleton's class was that he reported, not just class averages for each category that was tested in the fall and in the spring, but results for each each student in each category, one for the fall and one for the spring. The categories included the scores on the short list of so-called "reading comprehension" questions that had followed the silent reading and the composition-writing parts of the two, widely separated days. With those individual "reading comprehension" scores, one for September and one for March, it had thus became possible to see whether an individual student had scored higher or lower on so-called "silent reading comprehension" with the passage of time..

Those results from Waldo unexpectedly also posed a sort of "to be or not to be," on whether it is or is not possible to "teach" a so-called "skill" of the "experts" called "silent reading comprehension," without taking into serious consideration the meaning of that unending command from all grade-school teachers, "Pay attention!" Is that all that is really at issue, in the "teaching" of so-called silent reading comprehension, simply getting children to "pay attention"? The once massively used SRA cards, and the Thorndike-McCall Reading Tests, were supposed to improve silent reading comprehension. Children read those materials silently, corrected them personally, and then later went to other cards and repeated the same operation. Their scores were supposed to rise as they continued to teach themselves to achieve higher "silent reading comprehension." Was the only thing that was really achieved with all of that effort simply a better focusing of attention? An answer of "yes" to that question certainly suggests that there is no such thing as a "teachable skill" called "silent reading comprehension."

Children can get real educational results from reading assigned history books, or assigned real literature, on which their teachers can test them later, to see if they learned anything from their reading or not. If they fail their teacher's meaningful test, instead of something like a meaningless SRA card, then it would make sense to go back and re-read it. After they have concentrated on the material, they will have learned something useful, instead of a forgettable SRA test card.

Obviously, if the answer is "yes," to the question, "Can attention be voluntary?" then all that Miss Middleton needed to do to raise her scores would have been to run off a series of duplicated "reading comprehension" sheets to give to her class (like similar materials today and like the once widely used SRA cards). The sheets would have a little "story" or "article" followed by questions with a choice of possible answers for the children to check. The children's sheets would then be marked by the teacher and come back to each child to take home, many at first reading "F" for "failing." The next day's similar "reading comprehension" sheets on which correct answers had to be checked would then be handed out and completed. Amazingly, those next day's sheets would have correct answers checked by most children. Those sheets could then be marked, "A" or "B", to be brought home happily. Getting children to pay attention voluntarily on "reading comprehension" can be just that simple. I ought to know, since I taught third grade for thirteen years, and have marked untold numbers of similar materials.

However, the early twentieth century "expert" psychologists never taught third grade, so they came up with a different and far more difficult answer than mine to the question, "Can attention be voluntary?" My answer is an emphatic "yes," but their "no" will be discussed later.

The Miss Middleton Effect

It is evident that by 1915, because of Karl Douglas Waldo's 1915 thesis, and other testing being done, that the movers and shakers in education had stumbled across what can be called the Miss Middleton Effect, wandering attention. They obviously misinterpreted that effect, not on scientific grounds this time, but on their own personal, narrow, philosophical and religious grounds, exactly the kind which the United States Constitution rules are out-of-bounds in such places as government schools. (However, the Constitution, of course, never authorized the existence of government schools.) Government schools, for the most part, grew out of the French Revolution.

As indicated, Miss Middleton's combined third- and fourth-grade class was tested on silent reading comprehension in the fall of 1913 and in the spring of 1914. Also as indicated, what makes her reading comprehension scores so interesting is that they were reported, not just as class averages, but individually, by Karl Douglas Waldo in the January, 1915, Elementary School Journal (previously called Elementary School Teacher) of the University of Chicago. Because the scores were not only individually reported but were labeled, it was possible to compare each child's fall score to his score in the spring.

It should be remembered that children could read orally with great accuracy at that time when heavy phonics was taught, as Herbert A. Brown admitted in his article, "The Measurement of the Efficiency of Instruction in Reading," in the June, 1914, issue of the Elementary School Journal.

Children's high accuracy in reading words correctly at that time is also confirmed by the extraordinarily high spelling scores that were recorded in 84 American cities in 1914 and 1915. Those scores appeared in A Measuring Scale for Ability in Spelling by Leonard P. Ayres, published by the Russell Sage Foundation, New York, in 1915.

Karl Douglas Waldo reported that the third and fourth grade children he tested in 1913 and 1914 would have been been taught to read with either the Ward phonic system or the W. W. Howe "phonic method developed by [Howe] and used at Whitehall, New York." That meant that Miss Middleton's children had been taught to read by "sound" methods and should have been able to read automatically, just like the children Herbert A. Brown discussed in his 1914 article.

Concerning the actual "silent reading comprehension" scores in Miss Middleton's class, those of Miss Middleton's children who scored higher in "reading comprehension" in the fall of 1913 scored lower in the spring of 1914, and those who scored lower in the fall of 1913 scored higher in the spring of 1914. Almost no children scored about the same in the spring as they had done in the fall. Instead, the scores went up or down, sometimes WAY UP or WAY DOWN. Those scores can only be explained as mindless and senseless entries from students who were paying little attention to the subject matter. That, of course, indicates the existence of free attention, a faculty which is free either to focus or to wander.

Miss Middleton's reading comprehension scores are printed below. Note that it was possible for those children to score at 90 and 100% in their answers, which suggests that the questions were reasonable. Those other up and down scores only demonstrate an unwillingness on the part of those of the children to pay conscious attention. The following scores are only a small part of Table II in Waldo's study, which reported on all categories scored for the Third Grade portion and the Fourth Grade portion of Miss Middleton's class. Shown below are only the reading comprehension percentage scores for the 11 third grade children and for the 18 fourth grade children.

Only 3 of the 11 third grade students passed in September, scoring 75, 74, and 80. No passing third grade scores were reported in March, for which Waldo reported there was a possible excuse. For the 18 fourth grade Miss Middleton students, there were 4 passing scores in September, and 7 in March. However, only 2 of those 7 passing scores in March had also passed in September. Fourth grade student #3 had scored 90 in September and 75 in March, dropping in his score, and fourth grade student #15 had scored 80 in September and also 80 in March.

Miss Middleton's class certainly had wildly varying scores. With a third grade group of 11 children, and a fourth grade group of 18 children, for a total of 29 children, and with each group being tested twice, in September and March, a total of 58 scores was produced for Miss Middleton's class. Inattention to the test and therefore random chance presumably caused what were the huge number of failing scores, 44 failures out of a total of 58 scores, with only 14 passing.

Wandering attention must have been the cause of the failures because scores from September to March often did not increase but went down, often way down, and vice versa. Nevertheless, something like a bell curve does show up when all these mostly-failing 58 scores are graphed, because most scores cluster nearer to the very middle of the graph, and then drop off near the ends. That certainly indicates some influence other than random chance, the effect of random chance that is so very obvious on the European graph for Code 9, strongly phonic classes shown later. That European Code 9 "reading comprehension test" graph has no curve at all but is shaped more like the flat top of a table.

There must have been some use of the 1913-1914 "reading comprehension" idea in Miss Middleton's previous class sessions with her students that would have produced the semi-bell curve that suggests the use of some intelligence. However whatever those reading class influences were, they obviously did not lead the children to pay enough attention to the reading task, since it was random guessing that predominated in their choices of test answers.

### Third Grade

| Pupil | September | March |
|-------|-----------|-------|
| 1 | 16 | 45 |
| 2 | 75 | 35 |
| 3 | 74 | 40 |
| 4 | 35 | 35 |
| 5 | 33 | 44 |
| 6 | 33 | 38 |
| 7 | 40 | 40 |
| 8 | 0 | 25 |
| 9 | 48 | 38 |
| 10 | 55 | 33 |
| 11 | 80 | 20 |

## Fourth Grade

| Pupil | September | March |
|:-----:|:---------:|:-----:|
| 1 | 56 | 40 |
| 2 | 50 | 40 |
| 3 | 90 | 75 |
| 4 | 50 | 77 |
| 5 | 25 | 60 |
| 6 | 85 | 60 |
| 7 | 50 | 100 |
| 8 | 0 | 60 |
| 9 | 50 | 62 |
| 10 | 30 | 50 |
| 11 | 45 | 70 |
| 12 | 58 | 33 |
| 13 | 15 | 70 |
| 14 | 40 | 38 |
| 15 | 80 | 80 |
| 16 | 64 | 70 |
| 17 | 85 | 55 |
| 18 | 47 | 55 |

# CHAPTER 3

# Enter the Psychologists

A reasonable person might conclude that those higher-scoring children in Miss Middleton's class who later scored very low in "reading comprehension", or vice versa, were simply not paying attention, as we might read the newspaper vacantly and not remember what we read.

But you have to believe in consciousness before you can believe in true attention, because it is consciousness that pays attention. Furthermore, you have to believe in a free human will before you can decide that anyone can voluntarily choose to pay attention. Yet neither consciousness nor free will existed for most of the turn-of-the century psychologists.

How could presumably educated persons deny the existence of consciousness and free will? The answer, of course, is to be found in their materialistic "education." These psychologists had been enormously influenced by the materialistic psychology of Wilhelm Wundt of Germany, and probably by various materialists who had preceded Wundt, like Auguste Comte (1798-1857) the founder of the "positivist" movement. Comte had rejected religious revelation (and therefore rejected both Judaism and Christianity, the underpinnings of Western Civilization). As with Wundt's ideas, Comte's "positivism" was an influence on Thorndike, and almost certainly on James and Cattell (for Cattell, see Michael M. Sokal, pages 15-17 <u>An Education in Psychology</u>, 1981, MIT Press, Cambridge, Massachusetts).

Therefore, because of their materialistic philosophy, they had to reject the explanation for the Miss Middleton Effect which would have satisfied most other Americans. That satisfactory explanation would be that the reading comprehension tests showed that the children had paid little or no attention to the task, but instead demonstrated wandering attention. Only 2 children out of the 29 children showed consistent attention to the task, one scoring 90 and 75, and the other 80 and 80. It was possible for all the 29 children, who had been taught to read by phonic "sound" to read very well if they also concentrated, since that had been demonstrated by the 2 who did well. The children therefore had no need for the deaf-mute "meaning" method that was meant to improve their reading comprehension.

What is in contrast to these ridiculous tests is that no indication is given anywhere, in all of the "experts'" literature I have seen, that the 1914 era children were failing in the real subjects that were taught at school. Instead, there were reports of very high achievement in subject matter about that time.

W. S. Gray, the principal author of the first deaf-mute-method series, the "Dick and Jane" 1930 Scott, Foresman, had attached a long bibliography to his 1917 Ph.D. thesis at the University of Chicago. Gray's bibliography reported that in 1914 an article had been published by E. L. Thorndike on Thorndike's silent reading comprehension test. Thorndike's article had also included a report on Gray's initial oral reading accuracy tests in 1914. The tests had been prepared as Gray's master's thesis at Columbia Teachers College directly under Thorndike, before Gray returned to the University of Chicago to work under Charles Hubbard Judd, Thorndike's former classmate at Wesleyan. (Thorndike's 1914 article is also listed in an annotated Thorndike bibliography in the February, 1926, issue of Teachers College Record.) Thorndike's article was titled "The Measurement of Ability in Reading," and it had appeared in Teachers College Record XV, September, 1914.

With Gray's oral reading accuracy tests and Thorndike's silent reading tests given to the same children, it had become be possible, probably for the first time in history, to compare oral reading accuracy to so-called silent reading comprehension. It was most probably in that same academic year, 1913-1914, under Thorndike, that Gray formed his mistaken and negative opinion about the value of oral reading accuracy that he expressed in Chicago many years later. That was about 1940, and it was reported in Mitford Mathews' Teaching to Read, Historically Considered, (1966), in which Mathews quoted Gray.

Before all those tests in those 1913 and 1914 years were given, it seems likely that the "experts" would have expected consistency in the testing: the sight-word ("meaning") children would score lower on oral word accuracy, but consistently much higher on silent reading comprehension, while the phonics ("sound") children would score higher on oral word accuracy and consistently lower on silent reading comprehension. The psychologists were probably anticipating nice, neat relationships.

Yet it should be clearly noted that their deaf-mute "meaning" method to teach beginning reading, up to this point, might be presumed to be somewhat justified by Cattell's objective scientific experiments on the perception of printed words from 1883 to 1885 which seemed to endorse whole word teaching. It was only the psychologists' interpretation of these experiments that was wrong.

Their philosophical and religious biases seemed to have had no bearing on their endorsing the deaf-mute method. In 1913 and 1914, it seems apparent that William James' disciples, E. L. Thorndike, Charles Hubbard Judd and probably James McKeen Cattell (James had died in 1910) truly thought they could improve reading ability with their deaf-mute-method approach. (At that point, John Dewey does not seem to have shared Thorndike's, Judd's, and probably Cattell's aims in reading instruction, since Dewey had discounted the value of literacy itself as early as the turn of the century, considering "socialization" to be the purpose of the schools.)

In 1868, James had been the first to seek out WilhelmWundt in Germany. As quoted on page 93 of The Sane Positivist, the biography of E. L. Thorndike by Geraldine Joncich (and her title confirms Comte's influence on Thorndike), James wrote on May 5, 1868 in a letter to Henry Bowditch that he would go to Heidelberg because he could meet Helmholtz and Wundt there. Without too much effort, he could learn from Wundt about the psychology of the senses, which might be useful later.

G. Stanley Hall followed, studying with Wundt when Wundt had gone on to Leipzig, and before Hall received his Ph.D. under James at Harvard. Hall was an instructor at Harvard by 1875 and had been a friend of James before going to Leipzig in 1876. Immediately after returning from Leipzig, Hall continued his studies under James and received his doctorate from Harvard in 1878. Hall had studied in Germany previously but not under Wundt. It seems probable that James sent Hall back to Germany to study under Wundt before Hall received his Harvard doctorate.

From 1883 to 1886, James McKeen Cattell studied with Wundt in Leipzig. In Leipzig, Cattell continued the reading perception experiments he had begun at Johns Hopkins in Baltimore in the evening of St. Patrick's Day in 1883, in which both his professor, G. Stanley Hall, and fellow graduate students, John Dewey and Joseph Jastrow, were two of his subjects.

Many other American students after James, Hall and Cattell also made the pilgrimage to Wundt. Even those who did not themselves go to Germany were indirectly influenced by Wundt, such as Thorndike who studied with James and Cattell. What Wundt endorsed was pure materialism.

William James, Thorndike's professor in the academic year of 1895-1896 at Harvard, had been ambivalent on the subject of pure materialism, but eventually wrote an essay in 1904, "Does Consciousness Exist?" and concluded that it did not. William James wrote:

> "The word consciousness is just a loose way of indicating that certain sensory occurrences form part of my life history."

Concerning free will, for a 1908 book, <u>Essays Philosophical and Psychological in Honor of William James</u>, Thorndike wrote a chapter, "A Pragmatic Substitute for Free Will." Thorndike discussed free will in terms of instinctive responses and habits built on them.

Obviously, these views concerning the existence or non-existence of consciousness and free will should be filed under "religious beliefs" and not under "education," and should not, as said before, be allowed to have any influence on curriculum meant for government schools, where sectarian religious beliefs can have no place, according to the Constitution.

These psychologists more or less agreed with one another. In Cattell's journal on March 22, 1886, at the age of 25, while in Leipzig studying under Wilhelm Wundt, Cattell wrote, as recorded in Michael M. Sokal's book, <u>An Education in Psychology</u>, MIT Press, Cambridge, Massachusetts, 1981:

> "I am at the foundation a sceptic - the whole of my philosophy is 0.
> In the first story I have some metaphysical ideas, but don't think them worth working out. The sum of them is God, the world and I are one and the same.
> I really live in the second story and call myself a scientist. Here I am an atheist, a fatalist and a socialist, and make the world a logical whole albeit built on nothing."

In his "first story," Cattell was obviously a pantheist, but he "lived" in the "second story," as an atheistic materialist and socialist. All of these views were very fashionable, intellectually, in the 1880's. Many people, particularly students, have toyed with such silly philosophies in their youth but then rejected them as they matured and grew wiser. Yet Cattell apparently did not change his views with age.

Concerning Dewey's world view, he was reportedly also a socialist, although that by itself is an innocuous label. (Even Dr. Rudolph Flesch, who wrote <u>Why Johnny Can't Read</u>, declared himself to be a socialist!) Yet Dewey was no ordinary socialist, since he made a pilgrimage to the Soviet Union with Cattell and apparently others in 1928, Cattell having made the arrangements with the Soviet government.

(The source for this information is partly correspondence from Dewey to Cattell in the manuscript files of the Library of Congress, which was donated by Cattell's family to be in the public domain. Cattell later referred to their 1928 trip to the Soviet Union in a talk he gave at a dinner in Dewey's honor at the Aristogenic Society in 1933. Cattell's talk at this dinner is also in the manuscript files of the Library of Congress.)

Concerning Dewey's beliefs, in <u>John Dewey, His Thought and Influence</u>, edited by John Blewett, S.J., on page 34, Blewett told of Dewey's account to a friend, sixty years after it happened, of what could best be described as an emotional conversion experience to materialism. Dewey had said:

> "I've never had any doubts since then,... nor any beliefs.
> To me, faith means not worrying."

These "experts" had a Constitutional right to their beliefs or lack of them, including a right to their socialism, and a right to their devotion to Wundtian materialism. Yet they were forbidden by the Constitution to install a curriculum in government schools whose very existence was the product of their own personally held beliefs.

This is, unfortunately, exactly what they appear to have done. To continue to endorse the deaf-mute reading method, they would now have to explain away the wildly fluctuating individual silent reading comprehension scores, the "Miss Middleton Effect." The common-sense explanation for the "Miss Middleton Effect" was voluntarily wandering attention, or free consciousness. To reject that common-sense explanation, the experts would have had to build a different case on philosophical and religious grounds, and not on scientific ones, by rejecting consciousness and free will as the probable explanation for fluctuating "reading comprehension" scores.

Nor should this be considered a too-extreme view of their behavior, unless William James be considered too extreme in his views. On page 291 of his <u>Principles of Psychology</u> written in 1890, before he dismissed the possibility of true consciousness, James wrote the following. However, like Dugald Stewart in the early nineteenth century, William James was wrong in equating the will with attention, but he nevertheless clearly stated that the discussion of free will belonged in the "metaphysical" and not "scientific" category, since it concerned the possibility of "such a principle of spiritual activity." Therefore, William James himself identified the discussion of free will as a religious, spiritual question. I have capitalized the most pertinent portion.

> "...when we see (as in the chapter on the will we shall see) that volition is nothing but attention; ....we must admit that the question whether attention involves such a principle of spiritual activity or not is metaphysical as well as psychological, and is well worthy of all the pains we can bestow on its solution. It is in fact the pivotal question of metaphysics, the very hinge on which our picture of the world shall swing from materialism, fatalism, monism, towards spiritualism, freedom, pluralism, - or else the other way....
>
> "WHOEVER AFFIRMS EITHER CONCEPTION TO BE TRUE MUST DO SO ON METAPHYSICAL OR UNIVERSAL RATHER THAN ON SCIENTIFIC OR PARTICULAR GROUNDS."

The foregoing, however, should not be considered an openness by William James to traditional religion. On page 653, in his chapter, "The Perception of Reality," he said in a section headed, "The Influence of Emotion and Active Impulse on Belief":

"The reason of the belief is undoubtedly the bodily commotion which the exciting idea sets up. 'Nothing which I can feel like that can be false.' All our religious and supernatural beliefs are of this order."

In this second statement, William James defined faith as the product of a "bodily commotion" only different in its type from severe indigestion. It is also curious that, in this second statement, James contradicted his first statement. "All our religious and supernatural beliefs..." obviously fall into a "metaphysical or universal" category, and not a "scientific or particular" category. Therefore, as such, according to James' first statement concerning "metaphysical or universal" categories, the subject of "religious and supernatural beliefs" cannot be treated "scientifically" as he so ineptly attempted to do. Yet by the time James got around to making his second statement on page 653 about "bodily commotions" and "supernatural beliefs," he had forgotten all about his first statement on page 291 which had outlawed, in principle, the making of that second statement.

These early materialistic psychologists such as James, Dewey, Cattell and others are presented in the literature as the most rational of men. To understand them properly, however, they should be identified as implacable (and irrational) enemies of religion. Grave Constitutional questions are raised because of the enormous influence they and their followers have had on American school curriculum in all areas. This enormous influence has affected captive government school populations required by law to attend government schools in the absence of government-approved private facilities.

Metaphysical categories, however, should have been a problem for James on other grounds, since he had said, "Truth happens to an idea. It becomes true, is made true by events." In referring to the kind of philosophies on which James built that conclusion - the philosophies of men like Comte, Taine, Spencer, and Mill - Walter F. Cunningham, S. J., said on pages 67 and 69 of <u>Notes on Epistemology</u>, Fordham University Press, New York, 1930:

"There is a certain phase of Relativism which is at variance with our conception of truth, the phase, namely, that the human intellect cannot know anything that is fixed or absolute....

"Relativism, therefore, destroys all certitude and leads to universal scepticism; for it denies the absolute value of any principles; even metaphysical principles. Hence, no certitude, for all certitude, metaphysical, physical and moral, is based upon metaphysical principles or laws.... Consequently, Relativism is destructive of all science."

But William James, the Pragmatist, had said "Truth happens to an idea. It becomes true, is made true by events" (<u>Pragmatism.A New Name for Some Old Ways of Thinking, Lecture VI</u>, 1907). By James' time, in the late nineteenth century, Descartes' seventeenth-century sentence, "I think, therefore I am," ("Cogito ergo sum.") had atrophied so badly that the only thing left for William James in that sentence was "think." From it, James built his idea of the undulating "stream of consciousness" that contained both the ideas to be proven true and the "events" to be used to prove the idea true.

James clearly did not understand attention, either, any more than he did "truth." S. J. Samuels has pointed out that research has shown the brain to be a "single channel processor," which means that our attention can only be on one thing at a time. In other words, consciousness is indivisible. That this consciousness, or attention, can be free-floating, however, and is not determined, or automatic, or machine-like, has been quite clearly demonstrated by the results of research by Eric Klinger of the University of Minnesota. He has done research on what people are concentrating on at any given time, and done it in an ingenious way. His students carried "beepers" which, when they sounded, signaled the students to write down whatever they happened to be thinking about at that instant. A Discover article of November, 1980, stated:

> "After analyzing hundreds of questionnaires, Klinger concluded that a great deal of thought is unrelated to the task at hand. It ranges from fantasy... to mundane considerations.... 'If you define daydreaming as undirected thought, you could say that a third of our waking time we daydream,' notes Klinger. 'In fact, as I read the evidence, it may be our normal mode of thought. When we direct our thoughts, the remaining two-thirds of the time - that is, work with our heads in some deliberate, goal-oriented fashion - we have to make a special effort to do so."

So, we have to make a special effort, something we do with our wills, to direct our attention!

Yet these early twentieth-century psychologists denied free will and the possibility of free attention. When these psychologists had to produce an explanation for the startling and, apparently, unexpected scores like Miss Middleton's wildly varying "silent reading comprehension" scores, they could not conclude that careless voluntary attention was the cause. If there were no such things as consciousness and free will, there could be no such thing as VOLUNTARY attention. They did discuss involuntary attention - simply the response to stimuli.


How the "Experts" Explained the Miss Middleton Effect

Dismissing the possibility of voluntary attention, the "experts" must have concluded that the Miss Middleton Effect was the result of involuntary attention. Their explanation for the effect most probably was that it happened because of two contradictory sets of materialistic "bonds" for printed words. The defective set of "phonic" bonds was the result of "unfortunate" phonic drill when the children were first taught to read, but the "correct" set of "meaning" bonds had also been established in the beginning, depending on how much time was spent on "reading for meaning." Because of these mutually contradictory "bonds," the children's involuntary attention at upper grades while reading was presumed to be alternating between reading words sometimes for their meaning but sometimes only as sound.

The "experts" would have had a scientific explanation for the Miss Middleton Effect. Thorndike was supposed to have shown that there is no such thing as "transfer of training," so that all of the phonic drill in the early grades would not have "transferred" to reading for meaning, but would only spasmodically rear its head at upper grades to short-circuit reading texts for their meaning. (Thorndike was probably right about "transfer of training" but only when it concerns automatic, not conscious, behavior. When young, I was taught touch typing, in which the eyes never look at the keyboard. Decades later, during which time I had done a massive amount of rapid typing, I was amazed to find out that I did not know a good part of the keyboard visually. Without the keyboard in front of me to check, it was only by moving my fingers that I could remember exactly where some of the letters are placed. I had experienced no "transfer of training" from my automatic touch memory to my automatic sight memory.)

The "experts" obviously wanted to cancel the "Miss Middleton Effect" of alternating attention, which they seem to have assumed was swinging between word "meaning" and word "sound," and interfering with "silent reading comprehension." The "experts" probably thought, very sincerely, that they had a solution for that alternating attention problem, a way to guarantee constant, unwavering attention. That solution would be to install their deaf-mute sight-word "meaning" method, a method that forces conscious attention to meanings of words because it has to context-guess its way down the page. It absolutely NEVER deals with isolated letter "sounds."

Unfortunately for the "experts," some isolated phonic letter "sound" had to be used in 1911 even in the University of Chicago experimental school at second grade and above. That was because new vocabulary in reading books above the beginning level could not be reduced enough to do away with the need for "sound" phonics. For the deaf-mute "meaning" method to be perfected for use with hearing children above the first grade level, the vocabulary would have to be reduced enough, at least in the first three years, so that isolated, meaningless phonic "sound" could be completely dropped. Only "meaningful" whole-word, phony, "intrinsic" guessing phonics would be used, until a sufficiently large sight-word "meaning" vocabulary became firmly established. Children would learn how to use "jig-saw-puzzle phony phonics" pulling parts off different known sight words and putting the parts together to match a new word, which they could then remember by its appearance and its context meaning, not by its sound.

However, by the beginning of fourth grade, children would need to have accumulated "meaningful" sight-word banks of about two thousand of the highest frequency words (which would be more than 95% of any text). "Meaningful" word banks of that size would be large enough to permit readers silently to context-guess the meaning of most unknown words after that with the use of "meaningful" context guessing and jig-saw puzzle "phonics." Readers would then be able to read BY "meaning," instead of BY "sound," for the rest of their lives.

However, in 1911, there were no reliable lists of the commonest 2,000 or higher words from which to write reading books.

## The Sholty Study

Waldo's thesis is effectively buried today even though it must have been carefully noticed by the "experts" when it was first published. So far as I know, it has never been duplicated or even seriously covered in the literature. Waldo's thesis seems to be as lost today as is Myrtle Sholty's February, 1912 article, "A Study of the Reading Vocabulary of Children" in the <u>Elementary School Journal</u> at the University of Chicago which discussed the existence of two different and opposite kinds of readers. Sholty had done her research in 1910 or 1911, and found one little girl who could not use phonics, but only meaning-bearing sight words.

It was that very same year of 1911 that Thorndike started his word count of the 10,000 commonest words, which list eventually made it possible to publish the first true deaf-mute method readers up to the sixth grade level, using no phonic sound but only meaning-bearing words. With that large a list of the commonest words, it became possible to teach American readers to read just like that little girl Sholty found, reading only by meaning and not by sound. It is extremely likely that it was Sholty's study with the data on that little girl that prompted Thorndike to take on that awful, ten-year long task of counting words in texts, and recording his counts. It was his finished list of the 10,000 highest frequency words, in their order of frequency, that finally made it possible to produce the soundless, deaf-mute-method sight-word readers all the way up to the sixth grade level, so that all children could learn to read just like Sholty's 1910 or 1911 little girl, only by meaning-bearing words, and never by pure sound.

Even though both Sholty and Waldo did show up in Gray's 1917 bibliography, Gray did not report on what Sholty had really found, which was the confirmation of the existence of two different and opposite kinds of readers, (apparently automatic vs. conscious) that had first been announced by the German, Oskar Messmer, in 1903 ("Zur Psychologie des Lesens bei Kinder und Erwachsenen", Archiv fur die Gesamte Psychologie, December, 1903, Bd. H. H. 2. U. 3, pp. 190-298.)

In my 1981 book, <u>The Case for the Prosecution</u>, I summarized the value of Sholty's study, and am quoting that summary below. For the reader's convenience, the reading triangle diagram, from Suzzallo's article in the 1913 <u>Cyclopedia of Education</u>, is inserted at this point. Note that the points on the triangle can be used to illustrate two different movements (or conditioned reflexes) in reading: either the clockwise movement, from Visual (print) to Oral (sound) and on to Meaning, or the counter-clockwise movement, Visual (print) and straight on to Meaning, and possibly never going on to sound. That, of course, is the deaf-mute method.

\*\*\*\*\*\*\*\*\*\*\*\*\*\*\*\*\*\*\*\*\*\*\*\*\*\*\*\*\*\*\*\*\*\*\*\*\*\*\*\*\*\*\*\*\*\*\*\*\*\*\*\*\*\*\*\*\*\*\*\*\*\*\*\*\*\*\*\*\*\*\*\*\*\*\*\*\*\*\*\*\*\*\*\*\*\*\*\*\*

## THE READING TRIANGLE

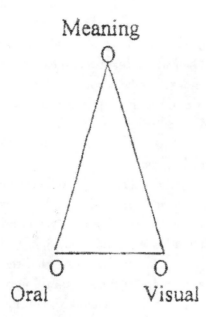

Meaning

Oral            Visual

Source: Article entitled, "Reading, Teaching Beginners"
by Henry Suzzallo, on page 118 of the 1913 volume of
A Cyclopedia of Education, edited by Paul Monroe,
Columbia University.  Suzzallo was also with Columbia,
at Teachers College, and had been a graduate student of
the psychologist, E. L. Thorndike, at Columbia about 1901
Thorndike had been a graduate student of the psychologist,
James McKeen Cattell, at Columbia in 1898, and of
the psychologist, William James, at Harvard,
before that.

*************************************************************************

The 1981 summary follows:

"The thing that apparently really sparked the change in reading methods and brought about those awful 1930 and 1931 readers of Gray and Gates was "A Study of the Reading Vocabulary of Children," reported by Myrtle Sholty in February, 1912, in the <u>Elementary School Journal</u>. Sholty's study really must have been a bombshell, which is why I am convinced that it was so effectively buried that no one today has heard of it. W. S. Gray "forgot" to mention it in the body of his famed 1925 summary of reading research to that date, just listing it in the index, with the wrong description.

"Myrtle Sholty had worked with three little girls half-way through second grade (in 1910 or 1911), flashing at high speed the 1,588 words they had been taught by then in their sight-word readers, which readers had been supplemented with diluted phonics in the University of Chicago laboratory school which the girls attended. Against their will at that time, the laboratory schools HAD to teach supplemental phonics or children could not remember enough sight words. Of the words the little girls could not read, Sholty found that two of the three girls were at least able to get the beginning sounds of a large percentage correctly. Yet the third little girl was unable to read words in parts but could read ONLY whole words. Nevertheless, she had managed to read correctly 977 of the total l,588 words, about the same as the other two girls.

"So the experts obviously concluded that she had managed to do without supplementary phonics (the clockwise route on the triangle, which route they so hated. The clockwise route stopped first at visual and oral [sound] before going on to "Meaning"). But they also knew that it is impossible for most children to remember more than a limited number of sight words without some kind of analysis, so they assumed the third little girl must have been using a different method, comparing a whole meaning-bearing sight word in her memory to another meaning-bearing sight word in order to tell them apart. Yet that was also the same as the visual analysis of meaning-bearing sight-words taught to deaf-mutes in Gallaudet's approach! So "intrinsic phonics" was invented which goes only the counterclockwise route and compares whole meaning-bearing sight words to each other in order to see like parts. Since "intrinsic phonics" always has to go through Meaning first, the meaning of the sight words, before it can get to the oral or sound stop, (if, indeed, it ever gets to the sound stop) they believed "intrinsic phonics" protected reading comprehension.

"Sholty was also impressed by the fact that all <u>three</u> girls, not just the whole-word reader, [when reading the text book] knew far more words in context than out of context. This showed that even those laboratory school girls who could use supplementary phonics did not use it all the time (clockwise) but sometimes went counterclockwise through Meaning (the context of the selection) for word identification.

"With the triangle plus Sholty's study, the mystifying remarks about "intrinsic phonics" and the necessity to read for meaning which were made continually by William S. Gray and Arthur I. Gates suddenly make sense. The triangle plus Sholty's study provide what Charles C. Fries in <u>Linguistics and Reading</u> (1962) said is missing in reading research, a thread of continuity of basic assumptions.

"However, the triangle and Sholty's study also provide an explanation for why they were buried for so many years. If children, going clockwise with phonics, are stopped on oral, and do not go on to Meaning, then other children, going counterclockwise to Meaning, may get stopped on Meaning and not go on to oral, the sounds of the words . They may, in other words, read inaccurately and spell badly, just as the phonics-trained children (or so they thought!) might not understand what they read but would read accurately. After all, Sholty did say, "The children who depended most upon phonics read with fewer errors than the one who read by word wholes." The triangle plus Sholty's study presented a distinct public relations problem to the early "experts," which they apparently handled by burying both the triangle and Sholty's study, as the public might not like the price to be paid for "reading with meaning:" which price is stumbling, inaccurate reading and bad spelling.

"The three little girls that Sholty worked with had been recommended to her by their classroom teacher. The girl who could read only whole words, called "A," was described as the best reader, and the other two as an average reader and a poor reader. The fact that the "whole word" reader was described as the "best" reader must have impressed those early experts, so they probably overlooked the fact that the teacher also said that Girl A was much below the average in all her other school work besides reading, "had no initiative', and "could never be depended upon to do a piece of work." Obviously, the poor little child could not read but could only guess from sight words! She certainly would not be able to spell, so how could she "do a piece of work"? Equally obviously, since ALL THREE GIRLS had to guess from context, that means that none of these University of Chicago laboratory-school girls back in 1911 or so could really read!

"In reading through their school readers used since first grade, Sholty found that Girl A scored 87.6%, Girl B 90.5% and Girl C 82.4%. So only Girl B, the girl who most used phonics, managed to score above the frustration level for reading of 90% (set after this study was done). Of course, that means she just squeaked through. After all, since these girls were only being asked to read the same reading books they had studied in school from first grade to midway in second, they should have been able to read them above the frustration level of 90% accuracy!

"It was obvious to Myrtle Sholty that these little girls represented two different kinds of readers: those who could see words in parts, and those who could only read whole words. Sholty immediately referred to a 1903 study by Oskar Messmer in Germany, discussed on page 92 of Edmund Burke Huey's famous and widely read 1908 book, The Psychology and Pedagogy of Reading. Sholty's reference to Messmer's 1903 work on the two different kinds of readers, which had been discussed in Huey's famous 1908 book, certainly suggests that the existence of two different kinds of readers was almost common knowledge at that time. That is because Myrtle Sholty apparently knew right away what her study meant and that her study had only confirmed what Oskar Messmer had already found, the existence of two different kinds of readers."

The "Experts" Could Finally Get Rid of Sound When Thorndike's List Arrived

Sholty's study had apparently motivated Thorndike to start his massive, ten-year-long word count so that in 1921 he finally published his results for the 10,000 commonest words. His succeeding in doing so, objectively speaking, was certainly an extraordinary and unparalleled achievement. Unfortunately, it had also made it possible to write the first deaf-mute method readers for hearing children, all the way eventually to the sixth grade level.

Therefore, by 1930 and 1931, the two original deaf-mute method reading series based on the commonest words were finally ready to be published. It had finally became possible to train future Americans to read only by word "meaning," and never by word "sound".

What is almost unbelievable is the extraordinary success those "experts" had in changing the behavior of our entire nation, so that now most Americans probably do decode texts consciously, by "meaning," instead of automatically by "sound. That is certainly implied by the research results on American readers which were quoted earlier, from page 11 of <u>Becoming a, Nation of Readers, The Report of the Commission on Reading</u>, The National Institute of Education, U. S. Department of Education, Washington, D. C., 1985:

> "The generally accepted current model of word identification [is that] a possible interpretation of a word usually begins forming in the mind as soon as even partial information has been gleaned about the letters in the word..... When enough evidence from the letters and the context becomes available, the possible interpretation becomes a positive identification."

It is worth repeating again: This model which uses guessing for word identification, which is based on actual tests on American readers, implies that automaticity is lacking for these readers, not just on unfamiliar words, but on almost ALL words! This awful statement confirms that the American readers they tested can only read print by the use of conscious guessing, just like partially deaf people trying to follow a conversation.

After the deaf-mute readers were finally in print, Thorndike, himself, gave the recipe for how pupils should read at fourth grade and higher. His very precise recipe appeared in his article, "Improving the Ability to Read," in the <u>Teachers College Record</u> of October, 1934. However, what is particularly attention-getting in Thorndike's 1934 article is the fact that he flatly stated that he, himself, would make no comments at all about reading instruction BELOW the fourth-grade level!

Therefore, it is very obvious that Thorndike meant to disassociate himself from the critical first three grades and to leave them in the hands of his ex-students: William Scott Gray, who wrote the deaf-mute method Scott Foresman reading series in 1930, and Arthur Irving Gates, who wrote the Macmillan deaf-mute version in 1931.

Those 1930 and 1931 texts and the others following them have succeeded in teaching most Americans to read by conscious guessing, "psycholinguistically", instead of automatically, as the whole rest of the alphabet-reading world had always done, for almost 2,000 years, until the unfortunate arrival of meaning-bearing sight-words in France in the early eighteenth century.

About 1913, the psychological "experts" had begun their silent reading comprehension testing to see what kinds of bonds were coming up. That made them very like the blind men examining the elephant, except in their case, they did not even have an elephant. That is because they were busy examining something that does not exist, a "skill" called "silent reading comprehension."

Eventually, school superintendants followed the advice of those "experts" and installed a bad deaf-mute method for the teaching of reading. Those superintendents never found out what an awful thing they had done by failing to understand scores like those from Miss Middleton's class. Her phonically trained class, who could read accurately, had actually demonstrated their ability to read automatically, to let their attention wander while reading. It is only readers with healthy conditioned reflexes in reading who can do that.

The school superintendents also never found out what an awful thing they had done by failing to listen to the inaccurate oral reading of the "meaning" trained classes, or to consider their very poor spelling, which demonstrated they were reading-disabled.

Indeed, Miss Middleton's 1913 and 1914 scores, which demonstrate the existence of wandering attention, do provide the necessary proof to indict the "reading experts" of her day and of ours for ignoring the obvious fact that such a thing exists as the ability to read automatically, with free-floating and voluntary conscious attention.

However, it was obviously for their own good that the "experts" never did dare to spell out plainly to parents and to the public what it was they were doing, which was ruining accurate and automatic reading and excellent spelling by children for the sake of their imaginary so-called skill, silent reading comprehension. The "experts" must have known that they might have faced some very unpleasant consequences.

James, Cattell, Thorndike, Gray and Gates brought into America's unfortunate schools the vast, workbook-paper-wasting and years-long teaching and testing of their non-existent, "skill," so-called "reading comprehension." Huge mountains of workbook pages have been filled in by America's children ever since 1930, writing their silent answers to the workbooks' silent "reading comprehension" questions, so that they would become accomplished "psycholinguistic guessers". Not only were forests of trees wasted making the paper in those workbooks, but so were huge amounts of schoolroom time wasted that should have instead been spent in learning real, not imaginary, subjects.

For over a hundred years, we have been doing things wrong in the teaching of reading, and we are far overdue in correcting it. Before the next hundred years goes by, we certainly should replace the "meaning" method by the "sound" method in the teaching of reading, and throw out the teaching and testing of so-called reading comprehension. That time can be saved for the teaching of real subjects: history, geography, mathematics, grammar and real literature.

A further worthwhile change would be to outlaw the control of education at the state and Federal levels because it is that top-level control by "experts" that has made the reading disaster possible. It has also made possible so many other educational disasters instituted by "experts" (the bad teaching of arithmetic, spelling, grammar, geography, history, etc.) We should remember it was a very top level "expert," John Dewey, who is associated with the removal of the fact-based teaching of history and geography in the grammar schools, and the replacing of those subjects with a fuzzy, wheel-spinning subject called "social studies." With social studies, it does not matter much that Columbus sailed the ocean blue in fourteen-hundred and ninety-two. What is likely to be more important in social studies is how you feel about that.

State and Federal control of children's education, which control is now so manifestly out of reach of the children's parents that it has become a topic for the TV evening news, should be replaced by local and parental control. Local control should also be used to dispense the public's tax dollars that are set aside for education.

## CHAPTER 4

# The 1914 Miss Middleton Effect Appeared in Some 1977 Research Results in Europe

The writer, a primary-grades school teacher, had a half-year sabbatical leave in 1977 and 1978 in which to study first-grade reading instruction in schools in the United States and Europe, to be followed by oral reading accuracy testing in second grades in those same schools. Second-grade children were tested in New Jersey in the United States, and in Luxembourg, Holland, Sweden, Germany, Austria, and France in Europe in their own languages.

Observed reading instruction in first-grade classes was rated on a code scale from 1 to 10. Code 1 was total sight-word teaching, and Code 10 was total phonic teaching, with mixtures ranging from Code 2 to Code 9. The ratings that were given were based on this writer's personal observation of the teaching in the first grades of the same schools where the second grades were then tested by this writer. No previous contact had been made with those classes or teachers. The writer and the teachers met for the first time at the classroom door on the day of the observation and testing. Appointments had graciously been made ahead of time by the education authorities in each location, at the writer's written request.

Scores were recorded, for each class tested in the United States and in Europe, for oral reading accuracy and for (oral) reading comprehension. Approximate speed of reading and observed reversals of letters were also recorded. The results of the research was reported in this writer's book, <u>Why Jacques, Johann and Jan Can Read</u>.

For this research, the writer had received permission from the International Association for the Evaluation of Educational Acievement in 1977 to use a 144-word selection, the first five of the forty items in Booklet 31, Reading Speed Test, copyrighted by IEA in 1969. Permission had been granted by IEA to use this short selection with the understanding that IEA would be aknowledged in any written material resulting from the research. The writer had the test translated, by a commercial translating company, into Icelandic (not used), Dutch, German, Swedish, and French.

After the research totals for whole classes were recorded and also shown in graph form, the totals for all individual childrens' scores in Europe, in all languages tested were also shown in graph form. Those graphs for so-called "reading comprehension" certainly demonstrate the Miss Middleton Effect.

In 1977 and 1978 when this oral reading accuracy research was carried out, America had two dominant reading instruction methods in use, the vastly greater sight-word use which focuses on "meaning" to decode, and the far smaller "phonic" use which focuses on sound. However, in Europe in 1977, the few sight-word "global" programs that were observed at that time were far more sound-oriented than the American sight-word programs. The rest of the European programs that were observed and tested at that time were definitely sound-oriented.

As already stated, for rating the teaching of reading in first grades as observed by the writer, she constructed a scale of Code 1 to Code 10. A score of Code 1 meant the heavy use of sight-words, and Code 10 the heavy use of phonics, with mixtures falling in between (Code 2 to Code 9). None of the European schools observed in first grades by this writer in 1977 rated a score lower than Code 6. (Current reports are that such a happy condition no longer exists, particularly in France.) The rest of the European programs rated scores from Code 7 to Code 10. The American sight-word, "meaning"-oriented first-grade classes observed by this writer rated scores of only Code 2 or Code 3, and only one rated a score as high as Code 5. American "sound" oriented phonic classes rated scores of Code 7 to Code 10.

In all, about 900 second graders in this country and Europe were tested with the test described above, a 144-word selection, the first five of forty items in <u>Booklet 3J, Reading Speed Test</u>, copyrighted in 1969 by IEA (International Association for the Evaluation of Educational Achievement, Stockholm, Sweden). As already stated, permission had been granted by IEA to use this short selection if IEA were acknowledged in any written material resulting from the research.

Even sound-based beginning reading programs in America waste vast quantities of time teaching so-called "reading comprehension." Yet in Europe, before 1977, even though the "global" method (sight-words) was sometimes heavily promoted, there was apparently no great emphasis on teaching "reading comprehension." Therefore, any influence from the heavy teaching of so-called "reading comprehension" should be absent from the 1977 test results from European schools. The results should show the natural differences between the "sound" (approximate average Code 9) and the "meaning" (Code 6) methods that were tested in Europe.

After all class results in each country had been recorded, individual student scores from all languages were combined into final graphs. Following are those graphs showing the results that were obtained for the "reading comprehension test" and the "oral reading accuracy test" for the total individual scores in Europe in October and November, 1977.

***********************************************************************

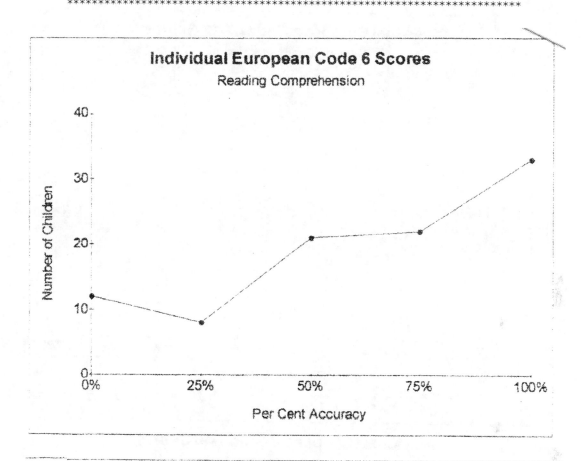

### Individual European Code 6 Scores
#### Reading Comprehension

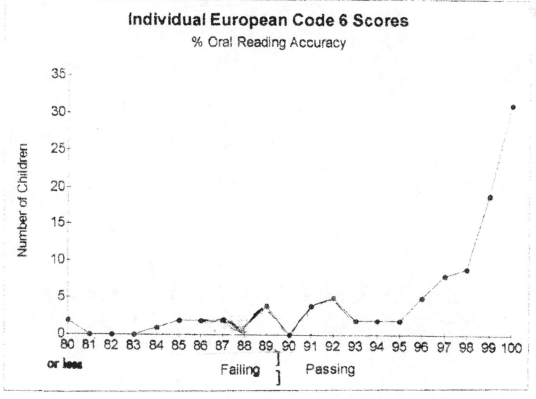

### Individual European Code 6 Scores
#### % Oral Reading Accuracy

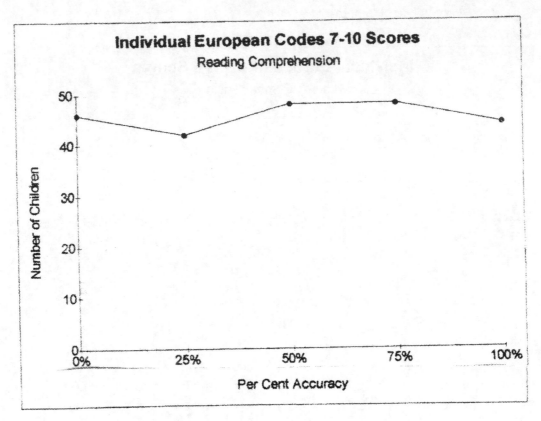

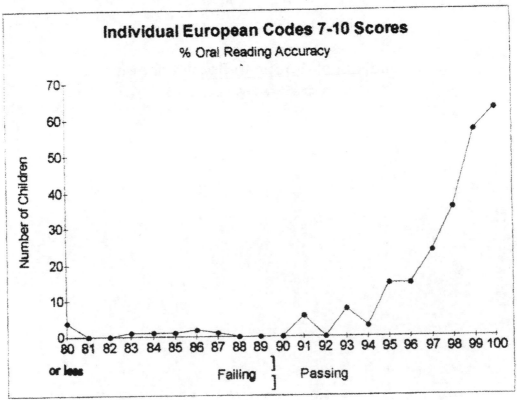

\*\*\*\*\*\*\*\*\*\*\*\*\*\*\*\*\*\*\*\*\*\*\*\*\*\*\*\*\*\*\*\*\*\*\*\*\*\*\*\*\*\*\*\*\*\*\*\*\*\*\*\*\*\*\*\*\*\*\*\*\*\*\*\*\*\*\*\*\*\*\*\*\*\*\*\*\*\*\*\*\*\*\*\*\*\*\*

One set of two graphs is made up from the 101 individual "comprehension" scores and the individual "accuracy" of oral reading scores of the children in the 1977 European second-grade Code 6 schools, where more emphasis on "meaning" in first grades had been observed.

The other set of two graphs is made up from the 237 individual "comprehension" scores and the "accuracy" of oral reading scores of the children in the 1977 European second-grade Code 7 to Code 10 schools, averaging about Code 9, where children had been taught with far less "meaning" emphasis in first grades and more "sound" emphasis.

Except for the observed difference in teaching methods (more emphasis on "meaning" or more emphasis on "sound"), the background of each group of children seemed to be very much the same. They appeared to be normal grade-school populations in each country.

The Code 6 reading comprehension graph has a normal curve, from very low at the zero end of the scale, increasing toward the 100% point. It has a normal semi-curve shape, implying that something real (presumably so-called reading comprehension) has been measured. Yet the Code 9 reading comprehension graph has virtually no curve and most resembles a flat table top. It is an almost straight line reaching across from zero accuracy to 100% accuracy. That is no normal curve. The contention is that it has measured nothing except the degree of attention of the test-takers, from total inattention to the meaning of the questions (0% accuracy) to total attention to the meaning of the questions (100% accuracy.)

However, attributing the higher comprehension scores of the Code 6 group to higher comprehension "skills" is the fallacy of false cause (non causa pro causa) when that which is not the cause of a phenomenon is taken to be its cause.

In both the United States and Europe, the higher averaged class reading comprehension scores of sight-word/global programs occurred uniformly in tandem with the other sight-word/global scores which showed decoding weakness: lower accuracy in oral reading, slower speed, and greater numbers of reversals. Therefore, the true, not false, cause of the higher comprehension scores of the Code 6 group was their poorer decoding which resulted in forced, but divided, conscious attention to meaning, part for decoding the words, and what was left over to answer the questions on the meaning. It was that forced attention to the meaning of the context which produced the higher scores, not better understanding of the meaning in comparison to phonic classes.

The huge spread in phonic comprehension scores of the Code 9 group from terrible to marvelous (from zero to 100%) cannot be caused by the phonic initial teaching method, since the Code 9 method's consistently high accuracy scores showed no kind of correlation at all to the Code 9 method's totally random comprehension scores. Those widespread phonic comprehension scores were the result of free, not forced, attention. That free attention could either freely choose to focus on the meaning of the selection or freely choose to wander.

Therefore, most of those 237 European Code 9 children in 1977 were doing just what Miss Middleton's 29 American children had done in the United States in 1913 and 1914. Most of them were just letting their free attention wander.

## Confirmations of the Two Messmer Types, Automatic and Conscious

It was in 1903 that the German, Oskar Messmer, announced his research which discovered that there are two different and opposite kinds of readers, apparently automatic vs. conscious ("Zur

Psychologie des Lesens bei Kinder und Erwachsenen", Archiv fur die Gesamte Psychologie, December, 1903, Bd. H. H. 2. U. 3, pp. 190-298.)

Myrtle Sholty confirmed Messmer's findings, with "A Study of the Reading Vocabulary of Children," her second-grade research reported in the February, 1912, Elementary School Journal of the University of Chicago.

A final table was prepared by this writer at the end of her 1977-1978 oral reading accuracy research in the United States and Europe, in which she had tested about 900 second-grade children. It very clearly demonstrated the existence of Messmer's two types, just as Sholty's 1911(?) research had confirmed the existence of two types. (The table. On the Consistent Profile of Arrows... also appears in Why Jacques, Johann and Jan CAN Read, (1979, 2004, 2008) by Geraldine E. Rodgers.) It is shown here on a separate page.

On the Consistent Profile of Arrows When Comparing Phonic Scores to Sight-Word Scores - Totals for the Second-grade Level on Oral Accuracy Reading Tests Given to 495 American Children in English and 338 European Children in German, Dutch, Swedish, and French
By Geraldine E. Rodgers

On the 1 to 10 Code Scale, 1 is total sight-word teaching and 10 is total phonic teaching, with mixtures from Code 2 to Code 9. Ratings were based on observations in first grades in schools where second grades were tested. The near-perfect consistency in the arrows' directions on this table, when comparing higher codes to lower codes, shows the presence of a probable force, a conflict between mutually exclusive conditioned reflexes for processing print: sound or meaning.

| | At or Above 95% on Test | At or Above 90% on Test | % Passing Comprehension | Estimated Speed | | % Reversals |
|---|---|---|---|---|---|---|
| | | | | % Slow | % Fast | |
| U. S. Fall 1977 Phonic Code 9.4 Compared to U. S. Sight Word Code 2 Sept. To Mid. Oct. | 58>37 | 78>42 | 57<63 | 15<26 | 10>0 | 9<16 |
| Europe Fall 1977 Phonic Code 8.6 Compared to Europe Sight Word Code 6 Mid Oct. To End of Nov. | 90>74 | 96>86.5 | 44<57 | 17<37 | 26>10 | 6<18.5 |
| U. S. January 1978 Phonic Code 10 Compared to U. S. Sight Word Code 2.9 | 77>53 | 92>75 | *51<68 | 8<15 | 35>14 | 6<11 |
| U. S. January 1978 Phonic Code 10 Compared to Europe Fall 1977 Sight Word Code 6 | 77>74 | 92>86.5 | *51<57 | 8<37 | 35>10 | 6<18.5 |
| Europe Fall 1977 Phonic Code 8.6 Compared to U. S . January 1978 Sight Word Code 2.9 | 90>53 | 96>75 | 44<68 | 17>15 | 26>14 | 6<11 |
| U. S. Jan. 1978 Code 3 Houghton Mifflin Compared to Code 2 Scott Foresman | 55>42 | 74>68 | 62<68 | 16<17 | 8<13 | 11<13 |

*Omitted 3 January phonic classes which must have fostered attention: 80, 82, 83, averaging 82. The other 4 phonic classes scored 50, 44, 56, 50, averaging 51.

A near-perfect consistency in the directions of the arrows on the table, when comparing higher codes to lower codes, shows the presence of a force in action. That force is presumed to be a conflict between established conditioned reflexes, one tending more toward automaticity in decoding, and the other tending more towards consciousness in decoding.

When higher code programs (more "sound" or automatically oriented) are compared to lower code programs (more "meaning" or consciously oriented), that consistent pattern of scores (arrows) appears. Higher codes score higher in word accuracy, and speed. Lower codes score higher on reversals and on that non-existent so-called skill, reading comprehension, the meaninglessness of which has been discussed.

The fact that the lower code programs score better in so-called reading comprehension really reveals that they have a forced, but divided, attention. Part of their attention must be spent on consciously decoding the words or they could not read at all. It is only what is left over of their attention that can be used to understand the text. Higher code programs read more automatically. Their attention is free, either to wander, or to focus totally on the meaning of the text. Without divided attention, they have the capacity to outscore lower codes.+

However, on the American scores, despite the fact that the phonic class averages were a little lower in so-called reading comprehension, when American individual classes at all codes were compared, it turned out that some of the American more phonic classes scored the best of all in so-called "silent reading comprehension."

While the comprehension scores for the American sight-word classes were higher than for the American phonic classes, they fell into a narrow band, higher than the worst phonic scores but lower than the best phonic scores. That suggests control from the method being used. Yet the American phonic scores spread out widely, from low to high, suggesting no control at all from the method being used.

The American phonic class scores in September and early October had one class average 31 and another class average 83, but that vast difference was hidden by the average shown for all phonic classes: 52. Such averages are obviously meaningless. In recording the January phonic scores, a different approach was used. The average that was shown was only for the dominant but sharply lower class scores: 50, 44, 56, and 55, averaging 51. The other three phonic class scores, which presumably reflect the classes' voluntary use of conscious attention to what they were reading, instead of the forced attention of the low-code programs, are 80, 82, and 83, averaging 82.

There is obviously a huge difference between the lower scoring phonic classes whose scores average 51 and the higher scoring phonic classes whose scores average 82. That difference most probably came because of the children's voluntary use of attention. The teachers of those higher scoring classes may simply have spent some time fostering that use of voluntary attention by such things as "reading comprehension" duplicated worksheets, to be turned in, marked and returned as failing or passing.

To summarize, this table, reporting the final test results on 833 American and European children, shows a near-perfect consistency in the arrows' directions when comparing higher codes to lower codes. That consistency appears to confirm the existence of Messmer's two types of readers, automatic or conscious, and the existence of mixtures of the two types.

Concerning accuracy in reading, it was possible for me in 1977 to test some sixth grade students in Sweden and Holland, and the accuracy was very high. Quoted below is a section from my book, The Critical Missed Step, reporting on those results:

"The great majority of those who learn to read by the "sound" method read at an accuracy level of 97 to 100%. When I did my sabbatical research in 1977, I took with me a portion of Psalm 104, Verses 10 to 18, in five different languages, which I had received, at my request, from the gracious American Bible Society. I only had the opportunity to test Dutch and Swedish sixth-graders with that short selection, and they were chosen at random from their classes. A Swedish teacher commented that the Swedish copy was a very archaic translation, but the children had no trouble reading it. For three Dutch sixth grades, (59 students), 97 % read it at 94% accuracy or above, 88% read it at 97% accuracy or above, and 61% read it at 99 or 100% accuracy, a large majority. For six Swedish sixth grades (56 students), 100% read it at 94% accuracy or above, 93% read it at 97% accuracy or above, and 73% read it at 99 or 100% accuracy, an even larger majority.

"In the United States today, most people learned to read by the "meaning" method. Listen to anything read aloud today. It will usually sound very smooth, if the reader felt secure enough about his reading ability to be willing to read aloud, but, if the listener has a copy of the same text, he will usually find it is read at considerably below 100% accuracy - most commonly at about 95%.. That is because the speaker is reading the text <u>by</u> its meaning, and not <u>by</u> its sound. The government study of American adults cited earlier demonstrated that those adults were consciously guessing their way down the page from the meaning of its context. They were not "hearing" the print automatically first, and only afterwards getting its meaning, which is true when we are listening to speech, and should be true when we are reading.

"The "reading experts" have had their way, unfortunately, since 1930, so that most of us are not reading automatically and effortlessly, as a computer reads, but are instead hard-working "psycholinguistic guessers." Therefore far too many of us actively dislike reading.

"Our impoverished curriculum, particularly in history, largely exists because students cannot handle demanding texts. Now even our country's history is quite literally, a closed book for great numbers of people. That is very dangerous, as ignorant people are targets for harmful propaganda since they lack the knowledge to reject it."

## Something Else About Learning Has Been Lost But Nobody Seems to Have Noticed

It is really surprising that no one today has noticed, because its importance was noticed as long ago as in Julius Caesar's day. W. J. Davies in his book, <u>Teaching Reading in Early England</u>, quoted from Julius Caesar's <u>Gallic Wars</u>, VI. 13,14, circa 45 B.C., on the Celts and their Druids, in what is now France. Julius Caesar said the Druids:

"...are concerned with sacred matters... A large number of young men gather around them for the purposes of education.... Once there, they are said to learn off by heart a great number of verses, and some pursue this training for twenty years. They do not consider it proper to commit these particular subjects to writing, although for most other affairs, both of a public and private nature, they use Greek letters... It often happens that when a person begins to place reliance on writing, he grows slack about the necessity of learning a thing thoroughly for the purposes of memorization."

So Julius Caesar thought that reciting aloud, purely from memory, was a far more reliable form of learning than just reading. No one seems to think that today. It should be pointed out that, in Julius Caesar's time, everybody read out loud, and not silently, but Caesar still thought that was not as good as memorizing. Yet it is probable, all across America today, that no one in elementary or high school ever proves that he has learned a lesson by reciting it (or writing it) from memory.

Earlier comments this writer made on this subject in Volume 1, pages 47 and 48, of The History of Beginning Reading, are appropriate here:

"The ancient practice of oral recitation of material to be learned was still around when Lewis Carroll wrote of such recitations in Alice in Wonderland, [Editor: 1865] but it is rarely to be seen in classrooms today in the English-speaking world. However, a watercolor drawing from a UNESCO calendar from a few years ago "The Recitation" by Tonje Strom Aas of Norway, showing a class of children reciting in unison demonstrates that recitations are still alive in at least one European country.

"A surprisingly worthwhile study on such recitations was carried out by, of all people, Arthur I. Gates. It was apparently prepared for his doctorate. (His doctorate was not prepared on spelling, as I had believed....)

"The date of the publication of Gates' doctoral thesis at Columbia (September, 1917), suggests Cattell's input since... Gates was living with the Cattell family and working with Cattell in the summer of 1917. Gates (and possibly Cattell) may very well have chosen the topic of recitations because of comments made over a century before by Dugald Stewart of Scotland, the philosopher/psychologist who wrote Elements of the Philosophy of the Human Mind [1814]. In a footnote on page 219, Chapter VI of Volume II of Stewart's work... Stewart said the following concerning oral recitation as a help in learning material:

"'It seems to be owing to this dependence of memory on attention, that it is easier to get by heart a composition after very few readings, with an attempt to repeat it at the end of each, than after a hundred readings without such an effort..,'"

An idea of Gates' curious and forgotten 1917 work, as forgotten as Dugald Stewart's is today, is given by the excerpts below:

"Recitations as a Factor in Memorizing, by Arthur I. Gates, Archives of Psychology, No. 40, September, 1917, Columbia University Contributions to Philosophy and Psychology, Volume XXVI, No. 1, The Science Press: New York.

"(Page 1)... It is at once obvious that the solution of such questions is of tremendous import for the work of the school. It is imperative that recall or recitation as a factor in learning should be analyzed and its quantitative importance determined... Earlier investigations have found in the case of many adults that the optimum combination of recitation and reading may lead to the mastery of a given lesson in one-half the time required to learn it by reading alone. If such findings should hold for children, and if it is generally true, as Miss Baldwin found, that twenty-five per cent or more of the pupils in the schools rely entirely upon reading in their learning, the loss of time and energy is appalling.

"The present study presents the results of an effort to answer a practical problem of the school-room - namely, What are the relative values of learning by reading as compared to learning by recitation in the case of school children working under school conditions and in the ordinary school-room methods of attack?

(On page 7 - referring to previous studies: "The general result is that for all materials recitation is a more effective method of learning than reading only.

(Page 93) - "Recitation, in brief, differs from reading physiologically by the fact that it selects and exercises the bonds upon which the established habit depends, while reading calls into action some bonds that are not strictly needed for recall, omits some that are requisite, and does not so well exercise the remaining few, needed for recall. Recitation is for memorizing what practice is for other habits. The physiological basis is the same."

Having written a worthwhile defense of "recitation" in learning with astonishing clarity in comparison to his muddy writings in later years, Gates made no further reference, to my knowledge, to this worthwhile material, nor, apparently, did almost anyone else. Nor, apparently has much been written on the fact that recitation is a form of "recall", and is therefore a stronger and more usable kind of learning than is "recognition." Recognition is the weaker kind of learning which can pass multiple choice tests. It is about all that is required of most students today.

Recognition memory is not real learning and, at best, is probably fleeting. Only recall memory is real learning. Julius Caesar certainly realized that, as his comments indicate. Yet recognition memory is about all that is required to graduate today, at most levels.

The result of the changes in education since about 1920, which were the gifts primarily of the early psychologists, is that we have students today with bachelor's and post-graduate degrees who could not have passed Waldo's tests in 1914 that were required for an eighth grade diploma.

# CHAPTER 5

# Unthink

On the Programmed Use of Unthink on Reading Instruction History

Unthink, the concept from George Orwell's famous book, 1984, is the single, most visible thread that runs through the events in reading instruction history. As in the Unthink of Orwell's story, the real facts have been deliberately distorted or have been deliberately hidden, and frequently both.

That was certainly true concerning Miss Middleton's class and all others like hers. The real story is that Miss Middleton's attention-wandering children, and almost all American children in 1914, could read very well. That was proven by the massive and very high Ayres spelling test results from 70,000 second to eighth grade children in 84 American cities in 1914 and 1915. Almost all children who can spell well can also read well.

Those carefully tested and recorded results were reported in 1915 in A Measuring Scale for Ability in Spelling, by Leonard P Ayres, a highly esteemed and even famous statistician. However, the Unthink distortion for Miss Middleton's class results in 1913 and 1914 was that the psychologists' silent reading comprehension tests had instead "proven" that Miss Middleton's children could barely read, with most failing terribly. They seemed to need immediate help.

By about 1931, the continued testing of so-called "silent reading comprehension" must have been revealing a seemingly "real" problem with phonic-trained classes because they could read automatically and so could let their attention wander. The sight-word trained children could not read automatically because they had to pay attention or they could not read at all. With their attention guaranteed, the sight-word-trained children therefore scored better on so-called "silent reading comprehension" tests

That is probably why most American government school superintendents by 1931 had finally adopted an inferior deaf-mute method for teaching reading (although they almost certainly did not know it was a deaf mute method), by buying the "Dick and Jane" Scott, Foresman, and the Macmillan equivalent readers. Oral reading accuracy tests for whole classes had disappeared (and must have somehow been made to disappear), so no one would know how badly children would now be reading because of the use of an inferior, silent deaf-mute method.

That veritable army of American school superintendents undoubtedly made the toxic change to the new reading texts without any understanding of the fact that they were buying a deaf-mute method, and a very inferior, silent one, at that, to teach reading to children with normal hearing. The method was certainly never advertised plainly for what it was, an historically highly objectionable method for the deaf, even though it had been the method used by Thomas Hopkins Gallaudet in his famous American school for the deaf in America, and by the Abbe de l'Epee in 18th century France.

That deaf-mute "silent" method was highly objectionable to Alexander Graham Bell, the inventor of the telephone, who gave lessons, himself, in 1871, to teachers and pupils in the Boston school that was founded by Superintendent Philbrick to teach the deaf to speak, to read lips and to read print. Bell's lessons were on the use of his own father's invented method, <u>Visible Speech</u>. Alexander Graham Bell's Scottish father, Alexander Melville Bell, had developed a highly successful "sound"-based method for the deaf, to teach them to speak, to read lips and to read print. Bell's charts even showed up in the movie, <u>My Fair Lady</u>, where they were used by the speech expert, Henry Higgins.

The deaf-mute "silent" method was also highly objectionable to many historically important others as far back as the eighteenth century, such as to the famous Samuel Heinecke in Germany, and to the Abbe Deschamps and M. Peirere in France, who had also developed highly successful methods to teach the deaf to speak and to read by "sound".

Miss Middleton's scores are, indeed, a frozen moment in time which prove the existence in 1913 and 1914 of automatic decoding of print as opposed to conscious decoding of print. The scores also prove that automatic decoding does result from the "sound" method to teach reading, since that is how Miss Middleton's children learned to read. However, the "reading experts" in 1914 and after must have misinterpreted scores like Miss Middleton's wildly fluctuating scores by concluding instead that they had "proved" that the "sound" method had failed.

The truth is that low "reading comprehension" scores on "silent reading comprehension" tests for phonic-trained classes suggest the presence of healthy automatic conditioned reflexes in reading. Such scores may result from the Miss Middleton Effect of voluntarily wandering attention while reading automatically. Yet the inferior deaf-mute method, because it forces attention to "meaning", may score higher.

The defective deaf-mute method to teach reading was being massively promoted by the "experts" of that day, some of whom were psychologists. By about 1931, almost all American government schools had finally followed those pied-piper psychologists and their "meaning" method, over the cliff and into the sea of functional illiteracy.

Because of the arrival of crippled, inaccurate reading by students, a massive change began to take place after 1930 in the school library books that were being published. Their readability levels dropped precipitously, but it is highly doubtful that the public knew anything about that drop in readability levels. Yet that massive drop in readability levels must have been carefully noted somewhere or it could not have taken place. Children's classic literature no longer was appropriate, because it had "uncontrolled vocabulary," which means sight words that children had not been taught. Instead, very inferior books with "controlled" very high frequency vocabulary were now being published as replacements.

Vocabulary growth for literate people has always been achieved to a large degree through their reading of books. Vocabulary growth for most children was now almost halted because most children could no longer read normal literature, but only controlled literature. About the bottom third of the students could not even read that. Yet there was no public knowledge of the cultural harm that was being done by the near canceling of vocabulary growth.

The story of the successful and semi-organized war on American literacy that was staged from 1826 to the 1930's and after has not been recorded, except in disorganized, fragmented bits and pieces that have to be reassembled with great care in order to tell the tale. That is in sharp contrast to the ethic of a far earlier time, the ethic followed by the ancient Irish annalists who wrote fifteen centuries before Orwell wrote his famous <u>1984</u>. In <u>The Story of the Irish Race</u> (1921, 1969), on the second page of the "Foreword," Seamus Macmanus quoted Dr. Douglas Hyde:

> "The numerous Irish annals in which the skeleton of Irish history is contained are valuable and ancient.... The illustrious Bede [of England] in recording the great eclipse of the sun which took place only eleven years before his own birth is only two days astray in his date, while the Irish annals give correctly not only the day but the hour.... These annals contain, between the end of the fifth century and the year 884, as many as eighteen records of eclipses, comets, and such natural phenomena - and modern science by calculating backwards shows that all these records are absolutely correct both as to the day and hour. From this we can deduce without hesitation that from the fourth or fifth century the Irish annals can be absolutely trusted."

That is, or course, exactly as it should be in any recorded history. McManus stated (page 352):

> "In history, Ireland's fame stands high. She was justly styled 'a nation of Annalists'.... Truth and accuracy were regarded as of paramount importance. 'To conceal the truth of history,' ran one saying, 'is the blackest of infamies.'"

Yet, as I wrote in a 1983 paper, and as is true in this work, most of the material I have included has had to be pried out of disparate sources, pebble by pebble, and then reassembled into the mosaic that is the history of reading instruction. That these facts were not sequentially recorded in reading instruction history long before I came along was the result of that blackest of infamies, Unthink.

## Sequential Examples of Unthink in Reading Instruction History

Change agents since about 1826 (not just since 1930) have worked to replace "sound" with "meaning" in beginning reading instruction in the English language, and to defeat any attempts to restore "sound" in beginning reading. This background has been covered at length in my earlier work, <u>The History of Beginning Reading, From Teaching by Sound to Teaching By Meaning</u>, AuthorHouse, 2001.

The following appears on page 488 of Volume I of my history concerning the change agents' circa-1826 successful removal, for beginning readers, of Noah Webster's superb syllable-based spelling book, which at that time was used to teach reading. Lyman Cobb was one of those authors, after about 1819, who had put out spelling books in an attempt to displace Webster's massively-used and enormously successful spelling book, by which children were taught to read. Those authors claimed Webster's was defective:

> "'Having pointed out... what I considered defective and contradictory in Mr. Webster's spelling book, I shall now conclude my remarks... by taking notice of some declarations made by Mr. Webster relative to his spelling book, in his appeal

"To the Public" published in New Haven, March 1826. Webster said, in speaking of the attempts to rival his book:

> "In order to accomplish their object, it has been expedient to depreciate my work and to charge me with innovation and with introducing a system of orthography and pronunciation in many respects vague and pedantic.... Surely if this is true, if my book, is really a bad one, I have been very much deceived; and I have done not only an injury but great and extensive injury to my country."

"Some people WERE in the very act of doing "great and extensive injury" to Webster's country and ours in 1826, but it was certainly NOT Noah Webster!

"Cobb said:

> "'...to my remarks on his spelling book, Mr. Webster attempted an answer in your paper [the <u>Albany</u> <u>Argus</u>] of the 12<sup>th</sup> December...'"

"In Webster's answer, he said he had supported his family on the small profits from his spelling book. [Insert: If ever a laborer was worthy of his hire, it certainly was old Noah Webster!] Concerning the argument on "correct" spelling and "correct" pronunciation, Webster said, when he completed his book in 1782, there were no authorities on spelling or pronunciation. Of those who had written dictionaries up to that time, he said something good could be said of almost all of them - except for Walker, whom he considered the most incorrect, but it was Walker's "authority" which Webster's opponents were citing as "correct." Webster's letter to the Albany Argus was signed, "New Haven, December, 1827."

So the opposition to Webster, including Cobb with all his arguments, fitted very nicely into the movers-and-shakers' apparent timetable for educational change in 1826 - which included government schools, teacher "training," and textbook control. These topics had been of great interest in the French Revolution, as shown by some French books published from 1789 to after 1793, cited in Volume I of my history, taken from the <u>Dictionnaire de Pedagogie et d'Instruction Primaire</u>, Paris, France, 1887.

Webster had felt it necessary by March, 1826, to write an appeal "To the Public" in defense of his spelling book against attacks. By December, 1827, he had publicly answered Cobb's attacks against his speller. But the change agents had won. Webster's sound-bearing syllable method for beginning readers was dropped almost immediately after 1826, and teaching beginning reading by meaning-bearing sight words replaced the syllable method in America and also in Great Britain, where other agents had been promoting other "meaning" texts.

It was shortly after 1826 that the change-agents had succeeded in their irrational, but complete, removal of the syllable tables from beginning reading. Of course, there had been opposition, but it had been powerless. The Boston schoolmasters had issued emphatic opposition, as recorded in many texts, but the movers-and-shakers had started to found teacher training normal schools, and soon began to hold two or three day long "teacher institutes" all over America. Therefore, the "correct" method now reached the teachers directly, and the children's reading texts had changed to the "meaning" method.

By 1840, state governments were taking over control of the local town schools, and the American sight-word "meaning" activists appear to have been in firm control at those state levels. The sight-word "meaning" method had triumphed. The French Revolution change-agents had certainly known what was necessary to effect that change: control the textbooks, start normal schools and special programs to train teachers, and put the government in control of children's schools.

In 1866, some 40 years after the circa 1826 cancellation of the "sound"-bearing syllabary to teach reading, John Dudley Philbrick, Boston, Massachusetts, Schools Superintendant, started in a very small way to promote the use of Leigh's phonic print ("sound"-bearing) in Boston primary grades, to replace the sight-word "meaning" method. By 1878, Leigh's phonic "sound" print was in almost uniform use in Boston primary schools, having been voluntarily adopted in each case. Yet, in September of 1878, after Philbrick had been fired in March, the sight-word "sentence" ("meaning") method was installed implicitly in Boston schools, by the wording in the September, 1878, curriculum, as the only approved method. The successful Leigh phonic "sound" method, like Webster's successful syllable "sound" method before it, had been pushed out of the schools, without any real public discussion. The correct method (Leigh's) had been labeled as incorrect, and the incorrect method (sight words) had been labeled as correct. Unthink had taken over the Boston schools.

The September, 1878, installation of the sight-word "meaning" method in the Boston primary schools followed the very strange theft of the records and "other school property" from the Boston primary schools in the summer of 1878. Almost all of those schools had been successfully using Leigh's phonic "sound" method by March 1, 1878, only six months earlier, at which time Philbrick was fired.

The theft is mentioned in a very queer comment which appeared in Boston School Document No. 6 of 1883, Committee on Examinations. In 1883, that official committee of the Boston schools had asked all the Boston schools to send them statistical data dating back to 1869. The committee made the following comment on page 6 of their May 22, 1883, report:

> "The committee were much disappointed at the imperfect returns received in answer to several of the questions issued. But many of the masters state in their replies that, during the summer vacation of 1878, the record-books, especially of their Primary Schools, were gathered up and carried off, together with other school property, and never returned. The books were probably destroyed, as no trace of them can be found.

> "The loss of these books is greatly to be regretted, as it renders it impossible to procure exact information, however much desired and important, in relation to the statistics of former years."

After that convenient theft of school records in the summer of 1878, no one would ever be able to compare the reading ability of the sight-word "meaning" primary classes of 1878 and later to the reading ability of the Leigh-phonics "sound" classes before 1878.

It is obvious that a change in primary school reading books had become necessary by September of 1878 because of the mandated (but only implicitly-stated) switch in the new curriculum from Leigh-print "sound" to sentence-method "meaning." The Leigh-print "sound" Hillard and Campbell primers (probably in the 1873 Franklin edition) which had been in almost universal use in the Boston schools in the spring of 1878 would have had to be replaced in September, 1878, with the Hillard and Campbell Franklin "meaning" primers in ordinary print,

The 1883 report quoted above stated that "unknown persons," who nevertheless must have had legal access to the many Boston primary schools, "carried off... other school property" in the summer of 1878, in addition to the primary school record books. Did that "other school property" include the Leigh-print classroom phonic "sound" charts and the Leigh-print Hillard/Campbell "sound" pupil texts that had been in use right up to the spring of 1878 when Philbrick was fired? If those phonic "sound" texts and classroom charts were gone by September, 1878, then even unwilling teachers would be forced to use the new, non-phonic "meaning" materials. Even if first-grade teachers wanted to defy the new 1878 regulations implicitly forbidding the use of Leigh-print, they could not have taught first-graders by the Leigh phonic method after 1878 if they lacked Leigh-print materials.

The 1864 Hillard and Campbell primer had a Leigh-print edition by 1866 as well as a standard print edition. For dates between 1866 and 1878, I found only those Leigh-print 1864 and 1873 editions of the Hillard and Campbell primer in the Harvard library stacks, when I was doing research there in the summer of 1986. However, for printing dates after 1878, the only Hillard and Campbell materials that I found were non-Leigh print versions of Hillard and Campbell's 1873 Franklin series primer. Those facts certainly suggest that there must have been a sea-change in methods in the Cambridge/Boston area in 1878, and that the use of those Leigh print primers was massively and suddenly dropped in the September of 1878.

Yet, as documented by surviving texts at Harvard, and as I discuss at length in my 2001 history, non-Leigh print Franklin first-grade primers had curiously been printed in 1877, the year before that 1878 sea-change, by University Press in Cambridge, the press used by Harvard, instead of by the publisher's regular press. That is despite the fact that the Boston schools annual reports seem to confirm that by 1877 almost no primary grades in Boston used non-Leigh print texts.

It is also probable that primary schools in the area adjacent to Boston, such as in Cambridge, also used Leigh print texts in 1877, or, through sheer chance, more non-Leigh print texts with publication dates between 1866 (the year the Hillard/Campbell 1864 texts came out with a Leigh-print version) and 1877 would have turned up in Harvard's stacks. That is because Harvard's collection of school textbooks at that time, and for many years afterwards, apparently consisted of donated books. The donors' names were carefully noted on a printed form placed inside a book's cover.

Donors obviously gave books that had been in actual use, and not books they had purchased directly from the publisher. Also, most donors were probably local, because of the relatively greater difficulty of shipping materials at that time, combined with the presumed minor importance of such a thing as a beginning reading book. Therefore, Harvard's collection of 1860's to 1880 beginning reading texts is a very good indication of what materials were actually in use in schools in the Boston area at that time. The surviving Harvard copies make it very obvious that Leigh print had been in almost universal use in the fall of 1877, but almost immediately disappeared, along with Philbrick, by the fall of 1878.

Someone associated with University press must have been remarkably far-seeing in 1877 to have arranged the publication of non-Leigh-print first-grade books for which there was virtually no market in the area in 1877, but for which there would suddenly be a huge market in September, 1878. That was when the post-Philbrick curriculum implicitly outlawed Leigh print in first grades. Yet the regular publisher always had non-Leigh print first-grade Franklin primers for sale if anyone wanted to order them (according to the book covers), so why was it necessary to have a special non-Leigh-print edition of the Franklin primer published by the University Press in 1877? That press had apparently never published the primers before and apparently almost never published them afterwards, except for that edition in 1877.

Was the 1877 printing done by University Press because it would have been impossible to order non-Leigh-print primers through the usual school channels until considerably after March 1, 1878, the date when Philbrick was fired? The firing of Leigh-print-promoting Philbrick had occurred six months before the start of the 1878-1879 school year, but it must have been far too inflammatory to place a publicly recorded, and undoubtedly highly-opposed, order for non-Leigh primers just as soon as Philbrick was gone.

In order to get the non-Leigh primers on time for the September, 1878, start of school, it seems apparent that the non-Leigh forces had those primers printed up quasi-surreptitiously, laying out the money for them ahead of time in 1877 from their own funds, instead of from school-tax dollars to which they might not yet have had access in 1877. Those peculiarly-printed non-Leigh-print primers were ready and waiting in September, 1878, right after the "other school property," which very probably included the earlier Leigh-print primers, had disappeared over the summer of 1878.

Someone associated in some way with University Press in 1877 appears to have been involved in a very sneaky plot. It concerned the probable removal of Leigh-print "sound"-approach Hillard and Campbell primers (in the 1864 and 1873 versions) and the Leigh "sound"-approach classroom charts from Boston primary schools over the summer of 1878. It concerned further the replacement of those materials with the "meaning"-approach, non-Leigh-print, Hillard and Campbell 1873 version quietly printed ahead of time, in 1877, by a press which had not been the former publisher's regular press. That former publisher went out of business sometime during 1877 and was replaced by a "successor." It certainly sounds as if there is another untold story that still lies buried, concerning the fate of that former publisher.

As early as Philbrick's 1874 report, he had said that Leigh print had spread to 31 of 37 districts in Boston, and he said that the Board "should adopt the system and make it obligatory in all the Primary Schools." However, I have found no indication that it was ever made obligatory.

Philbrick said on page 191 of his 1874 report:

> "The method of teaching the first steps of reading by means of the pronouncing type, invented by Dr. Leigh, has been used in some of our schools for eight or nine years. After an experiment with it in three or four schools for a year or two, an order was adopted by the Board, permitting its introduction where the district committees should choose to do so. Since that provision of the Board was adopted some six or seven years ago, no further action in regard to the matter has been taken. In the mean time, the system, without any compulsion, or pushing by outside agencies, has quietly made its way into nearly all districts...."

Superintendent Philbrick was no "mover or shaker" trying to control society through half-truths, so he reproduced only the bald, undoctored results of the survey he took in 1874 on the results from Leigh print. His results speak for themselves. Of the 31 Boston districts using Leigh phonics in 1874, 28 had used it long enough to form an opinion. Of these, the method was decidedly opposed by only one master, 6 had some reservations but were positive concerning it, and it was totally approved by at least 21 masters, or seventy-five per cent of the total.

Philbrick reproduced comments from the masters, such as:

> "The children learn to read in half the time it formerly took, and do not contract that old habit, so hard to eradicate, of reading one word at a time, as though they were pronouncing a column of words from the speller."

> "Pupils do four times as much reading; they read more intelligently; the vocalization has been greatly improved. Dr. Leigh's method had revolutionized the reading in every school under my charge where it has been well taught."

Superintendent Philbrick concluded:

> "From the examination of the replies of the masters, it is evident that the positive testimony in its favor is overwhelming."

Leigh print had over three more years in which to spread, and no evidence exists that it met any opposition from teachers during those three years. At that point, on March 1, 1878, Philbrick was summarily fired. Primary school records then mysteriously disappeared from different Boston primary schools over the summer vacation of 1878, which records should presumably have shown the excellent results from the widespread use of Leigh print.

By September of 1878, Boston primary teachers were implicitly told in the printed curriculum to teach by "meaning," not "sound," and such a directive also implicitly forbade the use of Leigh phonics. Instead, whole-word, two-step jig-saw-puzzle phonics was to be introduced gradually in the last part of first grade, just as is the case today with sight-word basal readers. Yet whole-word, two-step jig-saw-puzzle phonics is not real phonics. It is the same as the deaf-mute-method silent, visual comparison of whole, meaning-bearing words to each other in order to see like parts, so as to tell those words apart. The emphasis, obviously, is on whole-word "meaning," and not on isolated letter "sound."

Philbrick's firing was effective March 1, 1878, after he had been superintendent of schools, as shown by the annual reports, since December 22, 1856, with a brief period off because of health problems from September 1, 1874 to February 18, 1876. Only a few months after Philbrick's firing, the sight-word method was approved in September, 1878.

That meant the Boston schools were then copying the kind of massively publicized Quincy, Massachusetts, curriculum that had been installed by Colonel Francis W. Parker in 1875 under the Adams brothers, John Quincy Adams and Charles Francis Adams, Jr. The brothers were the grandsons of former President John Quincy Adams, and they had been involved in employing Colonel Parker as Superintendent of Schools in Quincy, Massachusetts. It was in 1880 that Parker left Quincy and went to Boston where he then became a Boston official for some time. After that, Parker became even more lastingly famous by employment in Chicago, or, as some of his critics might have put it, by disrupting education in Chicago.

Yet Colonel Francis W. Parker, who had been the Superintendent of Schools in Quincy, did not leave Quincy to become a Boston official until 1880. Therefore, Parker could not have written the anonymous 1878 Boston curriculum which endorsed teaching beginners to read whole sentences for meaning and which had rules which made it impossible any longer to use Leigh phonics charts at beginning first grade to teach letter sounds.

Neither does the Boston reading instruction curriculum which was published in 1883 sound as if it had been written by Colonel Parker. Instead, and very significantly, portions of that anonymous 1883 material sound as if they were written by William James, himself, whose writing style can be seen in his 1890 Principles of Psychology.

The record demonstrates that change-agents opposed any meaningful return to "sound" after 1826, once they had successfully buried the syllable method. They opposed programs such as the widely used phonic print of Dr. Edwin Leigh, Pronouncing Orthography (1864), such as the very popular Rebecca Pollard Synthetic Method of Reading and Spelling, 1887?, such as the widespread phonic spellers of the 1890's, such as the widespread supplemental phonics from 1900 to 1930, and such as any true phonic "sound" programs that have managed to surface after 1930. Those post-1930 true phonic "sound" programs include Mae Cardin's 1930's reading series. Mae Cardin had been either enrolled or associated with Columbia Teachers College but was so opposed to the sight-word materials being endorsed there that she left to write her own excellent phonic reading series. After the publication in 1955 of Dr. Rudolf Flesch's best-seller, Why Johnny Can't Read, many other true phonics programs came out. Yet none of them ever got much more than splinters of the government school market, where the "experts" obviously still had the most influence.

In 1982, Dr Patrick Groff of the University of San Diego reported in the March, 1982, issue of the Reading Informer of the Reading Reform Foundation (then in Scottsdale, Arizona) about the April 26-30, 1982, convention of the International Reading Association (IRA) in Chicago, the most massively influential group in the teaching of reading in America. (Samuel Blumenfeld discussed the founding of IRA in The New Illiterates and pointed out that William Scott Gray, the author of the 1930 deaf-mute-method Scott, Foresman series, had been one of its principal founders.) Twelve thousand people were expected to attend the 1982 meeting. A list of 400 separate activities had been given. Yet not ONE of those activities concerned teaching phonics!

Dr. Groff reported in the March-April, 1983, issue of The Reading Informer, Scottsdale, Arizona, (no longer published), on the upcoming May 2-6, 1983, convention of the International Reading Association at Anaheim, California. Three hundred fifty regular sessions had been scheduled, but only ONE concerned the teaching of phonics. The writer had the test translated by a translating company into Icelandic, (later not used), Dutch, German, Swedish, and French.

Dr. Groff's data establish that those IRA annual meetings in 1982 and 1983 were Unthink in action. In 1982 and 1983, many fine phonic "sound" reading programs were in print, even though the vast majority of American government schools used sight-word "meaning" programs with only fake phonics. Furthermore, massive statistical research data was in existence which confirmed the necessity to teach beginning reading by phonic "sound" (on which research data Dr. Groff had published many reports). Yet none of this massive pro-"sound" material was permitted to appear as the subject matter for any of the sessions of the 1982 IRA meeting. Presuming that the one recorded 1983 IRA session on phonics was objective (which is a very shaky presumption), then only one of the 350 sessions of the 1983 IRA meeting concerned true phonics. Therefore, the IRA programs certainly were Unthink in action.


## Concerning the Semi-"Official" but Fake History

Concerning the history of reading instruction in America, it is Nila Banton Smith's so-called "history" that is praised and cited by America's "reading experts". Her book American Reading Instruction, was published in 1934 and 1965. However, her bibliography shows a huge hole in place of some sources, when it is rearranged in chronological order instead of the piecemeal method she had used. It has only a very few largely-meaningless insertions in place of a fifty-year period in the nineteenth century.

Was it the influence from the Harvard "experts" that Nila Banton Smith was trying to hide when she left about fifty years out of American reading instruction history? That she did so can be demonstrated by arranging her 1965 bibliographical references in calendar order, instead of the order of the book's chapters, as she listed them. A rough review of her bibliography shows that from 1848 to 1894, a period of 46 years, she cited only 13 references, two of which two were European, two were Webb's sight-word readers, and one was McGuffey's. That left a total of only 8 other citations for those 46 years. Yet, for only the following 10 years, from 1895 to 1905, she gave 20 citations.

Specifically, between 1857 and an 1889 reference to Pollard, a period of 32 years, Smith cited only THREE American references. Yet, in the 32 years preceding 1857, she had cited 25 references, and in the very next decade after 1889 she cited 10, but, significantly, all but one were after 1894. However, Smith's references between 1845 and 1853 were also scant. In effect, Nila Banton Smith cut the half-century from 1845 to 1894 out of American reading instruction history.

Nila Banton Smith's gutted bibliography obviously had a purpose. It buried the reign of sight-words and "meaning" after 1826, it buried the failure of those sight-words, and it buried the phonic programs' opposition to sight-words. It buried the actions of the "experts" associated with Harvard in the 1870's and again in the early 1890's to see that sight-words and "meaning" remained in place in American schools. Also, in effect, Nila Banton Smith buried, by omitting, not only the influence of William James and James McKeen Cattell, but of G. Stanley Hall and the once-famous Colonel Francis W. Parker. She gave only two dates on Parker. One was on page 243 when she mentioned that 1901 was the date that the new Francis W. Parker School opened in Chicago, but Parker died the following year! The other mention of Parker was in her bibliography, not likely to be checked by a casual reader, when Smith gave 1894 as the date for Parker's book, Talks on Pedagogics. To someone unfamiliar with reading instruction history, that pushed Parker's influence beyond the date of 1894 and into the twentieth century, when the fact is that he died right after the turn of the century, in 1902.

Nila Banton Smith wrote her "history" at Columbia Teachers College when Edward L. Thorndike, William James' close friend and ex-student was still teaching there, and when William James' close friend, James McKeen Cattell, was still a neighbor and a close friend of Thorndike.

Nila Banton Smith's black hole completely cuts out, from reading instruction history, the 1860's partial return to phonics by the use of Leigh print in many places in the United States. It cuts out the use of Leigh print in the Boston schools for some 16 years. Leigh is not even included in Smith's index. Leigh's only citation is when his name is included in a list of writers who tried to indicate pronunciation by the use of markings on print. Smith wrote in the 1965 edition:

> "The Leigh, Shearer, Funk and Wagnell, and Ward System all made use of augmented alphabets."

In 1965, the Initial Teaching Alphabet (ITA) phonic print was in very wide use in the English-speaking world, so Smith had to at least mention the existence of augmented print.

Nila Banton Smith cut out what was the once-famous 1870's to circa 1890 Quincy/Boston group, with George L. Farnham, Johannot and Colonel Parker.

Widely-read education periodicals of the time, like C. W. Bardeen's <u>School Bulletin</u>, Syracuse, New York, reported on it all. Smith apparently ignored all those once-famous education periodicals.       ,

Nila Banton Smith left out completely the almost lethal market war that had been fought between the then-famous and widely used Appleton readers of 1878 and the revised McGuffey Readers of 1879, the latter being widely used only in the Midwest. That war had been reported in <u>A History of the McGuffey Readers</u> by Henry H. Vail in 1911. Vail had been a high-ranking McGuffey executive and had reportedly written Book One and the Primer of the phonic 1879 McGuffey series. The earlier McGuffey series had been non-phonic.

Strangely, Vail's 1911 history was not listed in the 1928 <u>United States Catalog</u> of books in print and was reportedly hard to get. It was about 1928 that the McGuffey Myth began to be promoted, so perhaps some "Unthink" tampering had been done on the <u>United States Catalog</u>'s records. Vail's work certainly provided a huge contradiction of the McGuffey Myth, which was that McGuffey's had nine-tenths of the reading textbook market in the 1800's.

However, Nila Banton Smith did not leave out just that textbook-sales war between McGuffey's and the Appleton readers. She also left out those once massively used Appleton readers, themselves, which were not in Leigh print and which used fake phonics. Of course, the very existence of the heavily-sold Appleton readers was an open contradiction of the McGuffey Myth.

Appleton's principal author was William Torrey Harris (1835-1909), one of America's leading philosophers at the time. Eventually, in 1889, he was appointed United States Commissioner of Education, until he resigned in 1906. The following is in the <u>Dictionary of American Biography</u>, Volume VII, pages 100-102, on Harris's earlier years:

> "In 1861, [Harris] founded the <u>Journal of Speculative Philosophy</u>... In it, such authors as ...Dewey and James... made their debut."

Harris's very early tie to William James is of interest.

It was Harris's massively used 1878 Appleton series, not in Leigh print, which pushed out from American schools the many other reading series in Leigh print. Almost all reading series had Leigh print editions by 1878, the year that the Appleton series arrived. Yet, by 1880, the wide-spreading use of the Appleton series seems to have effectively killed off the use of those earlier Leigh print materials

William Torrey Harris had been Superintendent of Schools in St. Louis, Missouri. His earlier history in St. Louis shows his connections with Leigh print and probably with Dr. Leigh. It was in 1866 that Leigh print had been used for the very first time, and it was in Harris's very own St. Louis elementary school where Harris was then the principal. (Since Philbrick is also credited with using it in 1866, in Boston, Philbrick may have been second in line after Harris.) In 1866, when Harris was a principal in that St. Louis school, Leigh was reportedly teaching in a St. Louis high school. Therefore, Leigh and Harris almost certainly knew each other.

St. Louis used Leigh-print editions of McGuffey's Readers for many years after that first year of 1866. Originally, Leigh print was used in the old sight-word editions of McGuffey's. When St. Louis received the 1879 new edition of McGuffey's with Henry H. Vail's real phonics, those old Leigh-print editions of McGuffey's were no longer necessary. St. Louis continued to use the Vail 1979 edition of McGuffey's Readers for many years.

William Torrey Harris fairly quickly became Superintendent of Schools in St. Louis but resigned in 1880 (possibly because of conflicts, considering the fact that St. Louis never used Harris's famous 1878 Appleton readers but kept on using Vail's 1879 McGuffey's). Since Harris's 1878 Appleton fake-phonics readers did not use Leigh print, its failure to do so had been an implicit insult to Leigh.

However, in her "history,"Nila Banton Smith totally ignored the widely-sold Appleton series and its famous author, William Torrey Harris. She ignored most of the many other widely-used reading series in print in the nineteenth century. By doing so, Smith protected the myth (and it is easily disproven) that McGuffey's had once been the dominant reading series in America. That myth was very useful after 1930, when the Scott, Foresman deaf-mute-method readers (Dick and Jane) really did become the first-ever dominant reading series in America, crowding out the many reading series that had preceded them, and remaining the massively dominant reading series in America until the 1960's.

The manufactured myth about the dominance of the McGuffey Readers began to be pushed in the late 1920's and was therefore available to pose as a fake and placating "tradition" when Scott, Foresman did become massively dominant less than ten years later. The Scott, Foresman 1930 series must have put out of business the great number of other reading series which had been listed in the United States Catalog, Books in Print, of 1928. Many reading instruction materials had also been listed in the United States Catalog, Books in Print, in 1912, and probably also in the unavailable 1876 and 1861-1871 editions.

Nila Banton Smith's treatment of the McGuffey Readers is just bulging with falsehoods. Smith's so-called history of the McGuffy Readers is scandalously wrong. That can be easily seen by checking Vail's account of the real history, in which Vail, personally, had played a big part. Smith ended her discussion with this comment:

> "...Mark Sullivan in his America Finding Herself (page 15) says that 'to millions, to probably nine out of ten average Americans, what taste of literature they got from McGuffey's was all they ever had, what literature the children brought into the home in McGuffey readers was all that ever came. Broad classical reading was not general. McGuffey, in short, because of the leverage of his readers, had a large part in forming the mind of America."

On that final massive piece of fiction, Nila Banton Smith left the topic of the McGuffey Readers and went on to discuss Tower's readers. The Tower series fitted in nicely with establishing her fiction that phonics had been in use in the mid-nineteenth century because the Tower series did teach phonics, but it was for elocution, not decoding.

Nila Banton Smith also left out any discussion of the once enormous Quincy, Massachusetts, education influence, active from about 1870 into the 1880's, and under the influence of the grandsons of President John Quincy Adams. The education newspapers and education magazines of that period were full of Quincy news on their progressive methods, so it would have been hard to miss by any real researcher, who would have been looking for such sources.

The 1878 Boston school theft and Nila Banton Smith's so-called "history" (1934, 1965) are only two of the numerous instances which demonstrate that William James' associates and followers were practitioners of "Unthink" in matters that concern reading instruction. Inconvenient facts were either buried or altered to make them more serviceable for their purposes.

The psychologist and publisher, James McKeen Cattell, obviously believed that the past could be buried. That is not only because he had been teasingly addressed by his close friend, the anthropologist, Franz Boas, as "Dear Censor" (in Boas' letter to Cattell of October 17, 1919, in the Cattell manuscript files in the Library of Congress). "Dear Censor" certainly implied that Cattell was fond of sweeping inconvenient facts under the rug when he could do so. Cattell's belief that the past could be buried was demonstrated by his 1917 or 1918 unpublished paper in the Cattell manuscript files in the Library of Congress which used a phrase from the Apocalypse in the Bible:

> "...We know something about the civil war - but the past of even fifty years ago is a book with seven seals....."

## The Burying of the Ayres Scale

In 1915, Leonard P. Ayres used his massive statistical data to announce that only about 300 words out of the half-million or so in English account for about seventy-five per cent of almost any text, 1,000 words account for over ninety per cent, and only some 3,000 to 9,000 words account for about ninety-eight per cent. These amazing statistics can be called the "cumulative high frequency word effect." Why then, did Thorndike ignore those statistics in Thorndike's own listings of the commonest words? Thorndike must have known those same statistics as Ayres from Thorndike's own, personal, massive word counts.

It was only because of the existence of the cumulative-high-frequency-word effect, and because of Thorndike's having identified the 10,000 commonest words, that it finally became possible to use the sight-word deaf-mute-method successfully on hearing children above the first-grade level.

The result is that even high-school students today can give the illusion of really reading when all they are actually doing is reciting memorized high-frequency sight words and context-guessing. Yet, so far as I have ever seen, Thorndike never referred to the amazing fact that so very few words, 1,000 out of the over half-million words in English, occupy more than 90% of almost any page in print. With visual memories of only those whole words, an illiterate can give the impression that he is literate,

However, the information on the cumulative effects from the 1,000 highest-frequency words had appeared very prominently, and with the most precise statistics, in the once-famous Leonard P. Ayres' 1915 A Measuring Scale for Ability in Spelling, Russell Sage Foundation, New York. Yet Ayres' scale had been effectively buried long before 1980 when I first accidentally learned of its existence by seeing a passing reference in a 1930's book. It is true that Ayres' scale is now available in reprints, but it appears to have been totally forgotten until some time after 1980. With Ayres scale buried, so was the fact that only 1,000 words are more than 90 per cent of almost anything in English print. Yet it had been that fact which had made it possible to teach reading by the deaf-mute method, once those 1,000 commonest words had been recorded.

Thorndike must have developed almost the same very precise statistics as Ayres did for each word of the 1,000 commonest words by 1921, through Thorndike's own personal, ten-year-long, count of word frequencies. Thorndike's omission of those enormously meaningful statistics for each word, not just of the first thousand commonest words, but even the second thousand, in his later summaries and apparently in his first summary, was a scandal in the field of scholarship. Thorndike did show the precise statistics, however, for each word above 2,000 in his last edition in 1944 and possibly in the earlier ones, so he certainly knew how to do so.

Apparently never publicly acknowledged has been Burdette Ross Buckingham's deliberate and unannounced harmful alterations of Ayres' 1915 statistics. Those alterations occur in Buckingham's 1918, 1919 or so "extension" of Ayres' 1915 A Measuring Scale for Ability in Spelling. Buckingham's alterations massively and falsely lowered expectations for spelling accuracy. Why did Buckingham do that on Ayres' carefully gathered statistics? Was it to help to cover the vast drop in spelling accuracy that is one of the effects from deaf-mute-method reading? It was Buckingham's gravely incorrect version of the spelling scale, not Ayres' correct version, that was used in schools all over the United States in the 1920's. That suggests it must have been widely promoted. Yet, after the arrival of the 1930 deaf-mute readers, the Buckingham version was apparently widely ignored. My copy of the Buckingham scale lacks a publication date, so I called Columbia Teachers College library some years ago to check the actual publication date. They did not have even a single copy.

In 1980, there were the torn stitches in the empty cover of the Library of Congress's then sole, surviving copy of the once-famous, but later-unknown, A Measuring Scale for Ability in Spelling, by Leonard P. Ayres in 1915. When I requested the Ayres scale in 1980 at the Library of Congress, I received that mangled copy. I then asked for and was given permission to look in the stacks. In the stacks were many copies of Ayres' famous handwriting scale. Yet there was nothing else in the stacks for the spelling scale except that empty cover I had received. Into that empty cover of the last surviving copy of Ayres' spelling scale in the Library of Congress in 1980, a copy of Ayres' handwriting scale had been deliberately inserted, with its own cover removed.

On that day in 1980, I also saw many little book-shaped wooden paddles inserted in the Library of Congress stacks in the reading instruction area. Each carried an intriguing title for a missing pre-1930 book on reading instruction. I never saw those little wooden paddles anywhere else in the Library of Congress on my frequent week-end visits in the 1980's.

In summary, concerning reading instruction history, not only has the knowledge and understanding of The Miss Middleton Effect disappeared. So has so very much else disappeared. It is obvious that Unthink has been applied.

As the accounts just described can demonstrate, a very damaged historical picture will emerge whenever anyone tries to make a serious inquiry into reading instruction history in the United States. Reading instruction history has been deliberately altered or deliberately hidden, and frequently both, as in the libelous charges against Webster's speller, as in Nila Banton Smith's "history", as in the McGuffey Myth, as in Buckingham's extension of Ayres' spelling scale, as in the successful hiding until 1980 of the real Ayres scale, as in the hidden theft of the Boston school system Leigh materials and test scores in the summer of 1878, as in the widespread fiction that America was largely illiterate before the arrival of government-controlled schools about 1840, etc., etc. and etc. Concerning that last fiction, the truth is that, before 1840 and the existence of government-controlled schools, America was probably the most literate nation on earth. That high literacy came from teaching reading by syllable "sound", instead of by "sight-word "meaning"..

The existence of that damaged historical record is no accident. Reading instruction history has truly been deliberately altered or deliberately hidden, and frequently both.

The ancient Irish Annalists' truism evaluates that situation very well:

"To conceal the truth of history is the blackest of infamies."

\*\*\*\*\*\*\*\*\*\*\*\*\*\*\*\*\*\*\*\*\*\*\*\*\*\*\*\*\*\*\*\*\*\*\*\*\*\*\*\*\*\*\*\*\*\*\*\*\*\*\*\*\*\*\*\*\*\*\*\*\*\*\*\*\*\*\*\*\*\*\*\*\*\*\*\*\*\*\*\*

APPENDICES

# Appendix 1

Teaching Deaf-Mutes, Experience of the Institution of Mount Airy in Changing from Sign Speech to the Oral Method, by Supt. A. L. E. Crouter, LL.D. (July 28, 1900)

From Volume III, page 1117 of this author's The History of Beginning Reading: From   Teaching By "Sound" to Teaching By "Meaning," 4/13/01, 1stBooks/AuthorHouse

From the July 28, 1900, issue of The School Journal, New York, an abstract of a paper before the Department of Education of Defectives of the National Education Association.

### Teaching Deaf-Mutes
### Experience of the Institution at Mount Airy in Changing from Sign Speech to the Oral Method
### By Supt. A. L. E. Crouter, LL.D.

From 1820 to 1870 the Pennsylvania Institution for the Deaf and Dumb employed the sign or French method, signs being the basis of all mental development and the principal means of communication. In 1870 articulation teaching was introduced, from thirty to forty-five minutes' instruction daily being given by a special teacher to such pupils as it was thought might be able to learn to speak and read the lips, the rest of the time being devoted to instruction by signs. Experience demonstrated the impossibility of securing the desired results under this method, and in 1881 there was opened a branch school where instruction was given by oral methods exclusively. At the same time two oral classes were formed in the main institution, the pupils of which were taught by oral methods but were permitted to mingle freely with the sign-taught pupils out of school. Practically all approved methods of instructing the deaf were then in operation under the observation of the same officers, by whom comparative tests were made at stated intervals.

In no instance were orally-taught pupils found inferior to the manually taught, and their progress in language was notably better. The work under separate oral instruction was found to be greatly superior to that done in the oral classes whose pupils were allowed to mingle with manual pupils. The speech and lip-reading of the half-hour articulation classes was less and less satisfactory the longer it was compared with that of pupils taught by purely oral methods, and such instruction was finally discontinued in 1888. On the removal of the school to Mt. Airy in 1892, the two oral classes of the main institution were merged with those from the Oral Branch, and since then only two methods have been employed, the pure oral and the pure manual.

The oral method has won its way in competition with the manual by sheer force of merit, so that since the establishment of the separate oral department in 1881, when nearly ninety per cent. were under manual instruction and only a little over ten per cent. under oral, the conditions have gradually reversed themselves until the enrollment for 1899 showed over ninety per cent. in the oral department and less than ten per cent. in the manual. Since 1892, only 20 of the 493 pupils entered under oral instruction here had to be transferred to the manual department because of inability to learn by speech methods, and their subsequent progress has proved that their failure was due not to the method but to defective mental powers.

After twenty years' experimentation with and comparison of methods the school has arrived at the conclusion that proper oral methods - meaning the use of speech and speech reading, writing, pictures, and the free use of books - are fully adequate to the best education of the deaf and that when a deaf child cannot be so educated it is useless to hope for any marked success under any other method.

# Appendix 2

Background on the 1870-1880's Boston and Quincy Education History, ibid, pages 576-589

Supplementary reading was Colonel Parker's special enthusiasm, and it was moved right into the Boston schools with the new curriculum of 1878. The supplementary reading which the 1878 curriculum guide endorsed for lower grades was the use of other first grade books than the official books, all of which had very limited vocabulary. However, with L. H. Marvel, Parker wrote Supplementary Reading for Primary Schools, First Book and Second Book. These had revised editions in print in 1882, according to Leypoldt's 1876-1884 American Catalogue. Harvard has a copy of the first edition of the First Book which came out in 1880, and it is a terrible thing consisting of very high frequency words and is almost devoid of sense.

What can be shown from the above curriculum guide of 1878 is that it made it impossible to teach Leigh phonics to beginners. Leigh's method required the use of his wall chart for rank beginners to learn letters and their sounds before being given words. Instead, this studiedly vague course outline in reading for Boston schools gave a casual emphasis on sentences. Chanting a sentence after a teacher had already read it can hardly be called "reading," but this is what replaced Leigh phonics for beginners. So, sight-word sentence-reading was moved in and Leigh phonics moved out of the Boston schools with NO OPEN RECOGNITION in the Boston school document that a major change was taking place! A table was included which listed curriculum at each grade level. In the last half of first grade, it showed "Spelling, by sound and by letter, some easy, common words from the reading lessons." Note that, in the last half of first grade, "sound" is used only on SOME EASY words in the reading lessons! Leigh phonics had obviously been outlawed for beginners without even mentioning it by name.

Under the section, "Spelling," on page 15, this statement is made:

> "Pupils in the upper classes may be led to perceive the few fundamental rules of orthography and pronunciation which belong to our language."

Being "led to perceive" was Agassiz's teaching method. He liked to leave a student alone in a room with a natural history specimen. Agassiz then expected the student to "discover" the truths about the oyster, or whatever it was that had been placed in front of him. Now upper grade Boston students were to be "led to perceive" the rules of orthography and pronunciation, which they would have acquired long before if they had learned to read with phonics.

The 1878 Boston curriculum was highly influential. On page 229 of the December, 1878, The Primary Teacher, published in Boston but sent all over America, this appeared:

> "...owing to the great interest felt in all parts of the country, in the course of study recently adopted for the Boston Primary Schools, which, is, in some respects, a "New

Departure" in this grade, we print the entire course in this issue of The Teacher. In subsequent issues, we shall furnish the courses of other leading cities."

The similarity between the specific lessons outlined in Farnham's 1881 book and the specific lessons outlined later in School Document No. 1, 1883, Method of Teaching Reading in the Primary Schools, Boston, "Prepared by The Board of Supervisors for the Public Schools of Boston," is striking. Both teach individual new words, as would be expected in the atmosphere of the time, from objects, but always in the context of sentences. Both then move to reading whole sentences. Both emphasize that the sentence is the natural unit, the 1883 material starting with the opening statement:

> "Reading may be defined as the act of the mind in getting thought by means of written or printed words arranged in sentences."

The 1883 report referred back to the Outline Course of Study of 1878 and was an obvious outgrowth of it. Any phonics, according to that earlier document, was to be held off until the last half of first grade, and even then it was minimal. The alphabet was obviously not taught before reading was begun, according to the table entitled "1878 Outline Course of Study - Primary Schools," and only a few script letters were given for copying in writing lessons in the first half of first grade and then used to copy simple written words. The rest of the written script letters were not shown till the last half of first grade. Copying a few script letters and words as pictures, with no reference to their sound, of course, had nothing to do with teaching reading by sound.

In the Boston schools which had so enthusiastically adopted Leigh print, there must have been great resistance to the 1878 edict, so the 1883 document included a section, "Phonics," which purported to allow its use after the beginning stage. When analyzed, however, it is nothing but elocution plus elaborate phony phonics. The real emphasis of the "Document" remained on "meaning," not "sound," as shown by the following at its beginning:

> "...The main point, therefore, to which the attention of the teacher should be directed at every step, from first to last, in the teaching of reading is this: Are the pupils led to get the thought?....

> "... When children are trained to utter sentences by merely imitating... there is established the vicious habit of uttering words without perceiving their sense, - a habit which is broken up later with extreme difficulty.

> "A written or printed word is used to recall an idea; it has no other use. A word which has been associated with a particular idea in the mind will, when seen, recall that idea, faintly if the association is weak, vividly if the association is strong. An association grows stronger by repetition of those acts which first produced it. A word is learned only when this bond of association has grown so strong that the word instantly at sight recalls its appropriate idea. It follows that the teaching of reading consists essentially in evoking acts of association between written or printed words and their appropriate ideas. That teaching which assists these acts of association assists the child in learning to read; that which does not assist these acts is useless.

If this be so, the best method of teaching reading will include all those devices, and only those, which aid efficiently in causing associative acts between ideas and written or printed words...."

It should be superabundantly clear that this was written by a psychologist in Boston, by 1883. (The overuse of italics is striking: William James was given to an overuse of italics in his 1890 psychology book. Note also the use of the subjunctive tense, "If this be so..." which had been common in ordinary writing before 1826 but was rare by 1883 except in the writing of highly educated people like William James.) Mitford Mathews thought Colonel Parker may have written this unsigned Boston report, but it does not sound like Parker's writing nor his ideas. Apparently, the only psychologists in the modern sense in the Boston area before 1883 were Hall and James (although Royce, for whom psychology was only a sideline, had arrived as James' substitute at Harvard for the 1882-1883 year). Hall was incapable of writing anything lucidly, and could not have written the above. Having read later material by Thorndike, James' ex-student, in which so much of the above vocabulary occurs ("bond of association"), and having read some of James' material which sounds so much like the above, I have little doubt in my own mind that at least the last paragraph of the above selection was written personally by James. Leigh phonic print had been thoroughly defeated by then, so the 1883 text could be more far outspoken than the 1878 text. It is even likely that substantial portions of the 1883 text had been written long before 1883 but that it was only safe to publish them in Boston by that date.

The 1883 report was a "teacher's guide" for almost all of the wrong approaches in the teaching of reading which have afflicted America ever since. Given below are excerpts from various pages. They are obviously drenched in "psychological" language.

(Page 7:) "THE WORD AS A WHOLE. Spoken words are learned as wholes. That is, there is no conscious analysis of the word into its elementary parts; or sounds, in learning to talk,. Indeed, most people use words all their lives without a conscious knowledge of phonic analysis. Again, in respect to written words, it is to be remarked that they are first visually grasped as wholes. Any attempt to see a part before the whole is seen only weakens the mind's power to take in the whole. A too early struggle with the parts of a word, whether spoken or written, absorbs the attention, and thus prevents the only act of importance - the act of association between the word and the idea - from taking place.

"The written word, to be effectually associated with its idea in learning to read, must be dealt with as a whole, just as the spoken word is dealt with as a whole when first associated with its idea in learning to talk."

(Page 8:) Under "The Sentence and the Thought," it read, "Words arranged in sentences recall ideas in their relations.... The use of sentences should begin after a few single words and phrases have been taught...."

(Page 18:) "...For the convenience of teachers a list has been prepared, consisting of all the words found in the first forty pages of the Franklin (new) Primer, in the whole of Monroe's Chart, and in the first forty pages of Supplementary Reading - First Book.... [Ed. Obviously, this was Parker's.]

"It is believed that from one hundred to one hundred and fifty of these words may profitably be taught in script, on the black-board, before the change is made from script to print....

(Page 19:) "...It is of the utmost importance that the words taught be thoroughly learned...."

(Page 25:) "...A few words, well taught, is a far better result than one hundred words poorly taught.

Immediately under this clear admission that sight words were being taught as wholes, came this seemingly placating section:

"PHONICS.

"There should be frequent drills on the elementary sounds in all the primary and grammar classes, varying in character according to the needs of the pupils. The Chart of Sounds here given for reference is nearly identical with the lists given in Monroe's "Physical and Vocal Training," an authorized book of reference. The chart, without the illustrative words, should be placed on the black-board in script at first, and later, when the children begin to read print, in both script and print."

The chart consisted of vowels and consonants marked very much like the keys in today's dictionaries. The children worked their way down the columns, imitating their teacher's pronunciation. Yet the report made it clear that, at the beginning of first grade (which is the critical part), a teacher was only to exercise the children orally on repeating words after her slow pronunciation, without reference to a written chart on the board.

The intent in many places giving such training was only to train the voice, but this 1883 report claimed the chart ultimately could help children to read independently. Yet the 1883 report, when read as a whole, makes it very clear the only "phonics" it was endorsing was phony phonics, Code 3 at the best. While it claimed to teach analytic phonics on long and short vowel sounds, it openly relied on "analogy," the comparing of whole words to each other, or two-step phony phonics, and provided lists of words on which to use such analogies. Page 18 of the report stated that "All the words... in the whole of Monroe's Chart..." were included in the basic sight-word list given to the teacher, so they obviously were to be taught as wholes. Therefore, Monroe's "phonics" chart was certainly not being used to teach real phonics, but only whole-word, two-step phony phonics.

Synthetic phonics was almost totally rejected:

(Page 29:) "In the exceptional cases, where children cannot be led to the pronunciation of new words by the analogies of the language, they may be helped by the use of diacritical marks. The premature and too frequent use of diacritical marks may lead to rapid word-calling, and away from the expression of thought, and should therefore be avoided."

The 1883 remark quoted above was the first clear and outspoken dumping of Leigh print in Boston, because Leigh print essentially consisted of diacritical marks. Aside from material written to promote phonic methods such as Leigh's and Pollard's, it is also the first of only two known references in American "reading instruction" literature to the fact that children learn to read far faster and more accurately with synthetic phonics than with sight words (with "sound" instead of "meaning"). At least two such admissions, however, have occurred in the European literature promoting the sight-word "global" method, one by Robert Dottrens in Switzerland in Au Seuil de La Culture in 1965, and the other by J. E. Seegers in Belgium in La psychologie de la lecture et l'initiation a la lecture par la methode globale, 1939 in Belgium, both of which will be referred to later.

The 1883 report also stated (page 29)

"The dependence upon analogy gives valuable training in language, and should be early and constantly encouraged."

The "analogy" to which it referred is Gallaudet's visual comparison of whole words already learned by their meaning, not by their sound: "bread, spread, thread," or "pin, tin, spin." E. L. Thorndike, James' student, wrote an article, "Word Knowledge in the Elementary School," in the Teachers College Record for September, 1921. It included a section, "Material for Phonic Drills," in which he showed "phonograms," or parts of words, followed by words which contained them, one of which was: "own - brown crown down town." (This was an interesting choice, as "own" has a second sound!) Since Thorndike endorsed only whole words, however, this was pure visual phonics, or two-step phony phonics, the comparing of whole sight words to each other to see like parts. However, as mentioned earlier, visual analysis of meaning-bearing sight words was common in sight-word books after about 1826. Its intent was very different from the grouping of like words by sound in the pre-1826 analytic phonics spellers, all of which words were learned by emphasizing "sound" and not "meaning."

Visual analysis compared whole words learned for "meaning" to new words so that the new words could also be memorized as meaning-bearing wholes. After 1826, such words were pronounced first by the teacher and not worked out by the pupil.

Yet, by contrast, before 1826, if Webster-type synthetic phonics was not used, phonic analysis was used by a pupil to compare parts of known syllables or words to parts of new words to determine the sounds. Words of similar sounds and spellings appeared in meaningless columns, and "meaning" had nothing to do with their arrangement. There cannot really be any doubt whatsoever that the old spellers using such analytic phonics were "sound" and not "meaning" oriented, since it was precisely because of all the old spelling books' lack of "meaning" that they were drummed out of beginning reading.

As is implied by pages 30 and 33 of the 1883 report, Boston beginners in 1883 were to be given in script, apparently on the blackboard, the first thirty-nine pages of the Franklin Primer, (apparently the "new" edition set up by University Press), "Monroe's Chart," and the first forty pages of Colonel Parker's unspeakably poor Supplementary Reading - First Book. They were then to change to print, as outlined on page 30, by practice from the blackboard. Afterwards, they were to read the following in print, not script:

"It is recommended that Monroe's chart be read first; then the first forty pages of the Franklin (new) Primer; then the whole of Supplementary Reading-Book First; then the Franklin Primer, from page 41. After these use the First Readers of the circulating supplementary reading books.

"Pupils should not begin the Second Readers until they have full and ready command of the First Reader vocabulary."

Note the reference to the Franklin Primer - obviously not in Leigh print. As discussed elsewhere, before the change-agents threw out Philbrick, the publishing information on copies of surviving primers at Harvard shows the change-agents had made sure they had non-Leigh editions of the Franklin Primer printed by University Press a year ahead of time so that non-Leigh-print copies would be on hand by the fall of 1878 when they needed them.

In this connection, a very queer comment appeared in Boston School Document No. 6 of 1883, Committee on Examinations. That official committee of the Boston schools had asked all the Boston schools to send them statistical data dating back to 1869. The committee made this comment on page 6 of their May 22, 1883, report:

"The committee were much disappointed at the imperfect returns received in answer to several of the questions issued. But many of the masters state in their replies that, during the summer vacation of 1878, the record-books, especially of their Primary Schools, were gathered up and carried off, together with other school property, and never returned. The books were probably destroyed, as no trace of them can be found.

"The loss of these books is greatly to be regretted, as it renders it impossible to procure exact information, however much desired and important, in relation to the statistics of former years."

Philbrick had been fired some six months before these record books disappeared. Leigh-print primers were obviously replaced with the "new" Franklin Primers in ordinary print in September of 1878. However, after the convenient theft of the primary school records in the summer of 1878, no one would ever be able to compare the sight-word primary classes of 1878 and later to the Leigh-phonics classes before 1878.

A further possibility might be considered: Did the other school property that was "carried off" in the summer of 1878 by unknown persons, who apparently had legal access to the Boston primary schools, possibly include the Leigh classroom phonic charts and the Leigh-print Hillard/Campbell texts that had been used right up to the spring of 1878 when Philbrick was fired? If those phonic texts and charts were gone by September, 1878, even unwilling teachers would be forced to use the new, non-phonic materials.

This School Document No. 1 - 1883, Method of Teaching Reading in the Primary School, "Prepared by the Board of Supervisors, for the Public Schools of Boston" is the single most important text ever published in this country on the teaching of reading. Its influence has been massive. It provided the formula and the philosophical justification for every one of the dominent reading programs used in this country ever since. Even Gates' and Gray's deaf-mute readers were ultimate elaborations on the ideas it contained.

Its roots, of course, lay in Gallaudet's deaf-mute method, which used a visual "phony phonics," but the document incorporated a far more elaborate phony phonics in the pattern followed ever since, even by Gates and Gray. Its elaborate phony phonics was also possibly inspired by Code 3 contemporary texts from England, discussed later, but the philosophical justification behind all of its recommendations is pure psychological jargon.

In my opinion, the ideas and even some of the phrasings which School Document No. 1 - 1883 contained show the clear influence of that very earliest American experimental psychologist, William James, though it is abundantly clear that the move to "meaning" in the Boston schools had to be the result of work by a determined group of activists, and certainly not by one man alone. The record suggests the activists were the disciples of Agassiz, who had died in 1873.

The record also suggests that these activists included the "philosophers" spoken of in the 1871 Boston school report, mentioned in a quotation given below, who were enormously disapproving of Leigh phonics, and William James was a philosopher, even in his youth. James' work was first published in a journal edited by William Torrey Harris, mentioned elsewhere. It is an intriguing fact that America's leading philosopher at the time, William Torrey Harris, was the principal author on the massively used 1878 Appleton series, which had no Leigh-print edition and which was primarily responsible for pushing the earlier reading series in Leigh print out of American schools.

William James was unemployed in 1870 and the usual references to this period in his life, after he received his doctorate in 1869 and began teaching at Harvard in 1872, is that he was in a state of nervous semi-collapse. That is a very long nervous collapse, to put it mildly: from 27 to 30 years of age. He undoubtedly shared his family's tendencies to hypochondria, but could act when he saw fit. On page 20 of Leon Edel's biography of Henry James, Edel referred to a letter Henry James wrote Charles Eliot Norton shortly after Henry James returned to America in May, 1870. Henry James mentioned William James' activities, and his comments suggest that his brother was very well in the late spring of 1870, despite William's famous and frightening psychic experience in March of 1870 (quoted, for instance in William James, a Biography, by Gay Wilson Allen, page 166. His father, who became a Swedenborgian afterwards, had had a similar horrifying psychic experience many years before.) Concerning William James' activities in the late spring of 1870, Edel said William James had finished his medical training, and according to Henry James' comments in his letter to Norton, was mixing with intellectual young men who had started a metaphysical club, in which they argued humorlessly and stayed to the topic chosen. Henry wrote that just to think of their activities gave him a headache.

According to Allen's biography on page 168, William James wrote in his diary on April 30 that he had passed a crisis in his life the day before, and had determined to believe in free will. For the rest of the year, he intended to avoid speculating, and would concentrate on moral freedom, by reading books supporting it, and by his actions. After the beginning of the next year, he felt he might return to his philosophical studies of skepticism without having such studies interfere with his ability to act.

Allen wrote concerning the period after May, 1870, on page 172:

"During this period when both William and Henry were at home in Cambridge, William was not writing many letters, and therefore documentary evidence for this year in his life is scarce. He was not even keeping his diary, but this is a good indication that he was successfully avoiding emotional stress, for it was during periods of strain and crisis that he wrote most copiously in his diary."

Therefore, during the most of 1870, when Farnham was first using the sentence method, James was healthy and in a frame of mind to "act."

William James had been a student of Agassiz of Harvard, who, for a few years before his death in 1873, had urged his followers to go out and do something about education. James Johonnot, who wrote Principles and Practice of Teaching in 1878 included a chapter on Louis Agassiz, the Harvard biologist whose expedition to the Amazon in 1865 William James had joined. Johonnot had attended Agassiz's famed natural history course at Penikese Island off Massachusetts in the summer of 1873, just before Agassiz's death. Johonnot wrote:

"The life of 'the master,' as he was affectionately called by his pupils, was cut short at the very commencement of this most important enterprise of his life, and it is left to others to carry on to a successful termination the work he had begun...."

Concerning Agassiz's "enterprise," Johonnot had said earlier, as previously quoted in part:

"(Agassiz) saw that, in the prevailing education, language largely took the place of thought; that more attention was given to the symbols of knowledge than to the knowledge itself....

"Those errors, he saw, could be corrected only by a radical and fundamental change in the whole system of education, in which the scientific spirit and methods should play a prominent part. He commenced the work of reform with his characteristic caution and energy, calling attention to some of the prominent defects of education in his public lectures.... His success was so great, that he resolved to try and reach the public schools by instruction offered to teachers...." (at Penikese in 1873).

That Agassiz was campaigning for major changes in education in the school year 1870-1871 is evident from Philbrick's comments. In the Annual Report of the School Committee of the City of Boston - 1871 for the school year 1870-1871, on page 142, Philbrick said:

"I find around me conflicting opinions, not only as to what should be the aim in education, but also on the details of means and methods. I am often button-holed and lectured by persons holding opposite and extreme, and, what seem to me, one-sided views on educational matters. In this way,

I am sometimes entertained and instructed, and sometimes not. I am, on the whole, rather fond of hearing what the enthusiast and the man of one idea has to say."

He outlined his experiences in a number of such encounters, and then said, on page 149:

"Being an honest seeker of truth, or at least imagining myself to be such, and appreciating very highly the privilege of listening to the instruction of learned and wise men, I make a point of attending a meeting where a truly great man is to speak to teachers on education. I am charmed and edified with what he says of the importance and the ways and means of teaching in our elementary schools the rudiments of natural science. EVERY PRIMARY SCHOOL, HE SAYS MUST HAVE ITS LITTLE MUSEUM OF NATURAL HISTORY. That sentence I felt sure would live and be quoted the world over, for he who uttered it was the very best authority in such a matter. He then goes on to depreciate the value of the study of words, and finally declares that the study of English Grammar should be abolished as a useless waste of time. Here the query naturally arose, whether a man who was an acknowledged authority in one department of learning is equally entitled to respect as an authority in those branches which are outside his specialty?"

There can be no question that Philbrick was referring to Louis Agassiz, and that fact is confirmed by Johonnot's comments. Therefore, Agassiz (the idol of a near cult, eventually, as Johonnot made clear) was publicly downgrading in lectures the value of "words" in education, during the school year 1870-1871, the same school year that Farnham introduced the sentence method into Binghamton, which method could eventually be "justified" by William James' sentence "stream of consciousness" ideas which would only come out in print in his psychology book of 1890. That year, 1870, was also the same year that John Quincy Adams, Jr., chose to join the Quincy school board, with the presumed desire to aid education.

It is probable Agassiz' proselytizing had something to do with the winds for change blowing in Quincy, through the actions of the Adams' brothers, starting with John Quincy Adams' school committee membership in 1870 and that of his brother, Charles Francis Adams, Jr., by 1872.

It is very clear that Charles Francis Adams, Jr., agreed with Agassiz on the uselessness of teaching much grammar. Charles Francis Adams, Jr., was on the Quincy School Committee in 1872-1873, two years before it hired Colonel Parker. In the Harvard copy of the Report of the School Committee of the Town of Quincy for the School Year 1872-73, someone has put an asterisk after the word, "me" in the following sentence on page 14, and, at the bottom of the page, written in pencil in an old-fashioned script, "C.F. Adams, Jr." Here is that sentence and some of the comments which followed, a portion of which has been quoted previously:

"Under the division of duties during the past year, the examination of all the schools in grammar was assigned to me. As a general conclusion from my observations during that time, I am compelled to say, that, although there is abundant evidence of much honest labor and drilling on the part both of instructors and scholars, yet, as now taught in our schools, English grammar is a singularly unprofitable branch of instruction. The children are indeed taught the names of the parts of speech, and are drilled to parse the words of an ordinary sentence, - in the better schools they may even attain to some slight knowledge of analysis. I am, however, wholly unable to see that this labor at present results in any thing more than a dry, useless, and unattractive mental discipline. This I do not understand to be the object of a common-school education, in which utility is the one end which should always be kept in view...."

Adams was obviously not endorsing the idea that all men should have access to all wholesome knowledge, or that such learning is, of and by itself, a good thing, or that the human mind hungers after truth for its own sake just as the human body hungers after food. Adams' ideas on the "utility" of the kind of education that should be available for ordinary citizens sounds uncomfortably like the old marauding Vikings' practice known as the drowning of the books.

Adams continued:

"In this respect, an immediate reform is called for....

"The object of studying English grammar is to learn how to speak and write the English language correctly... The fact is, nevertheless, apparent, that the study of grammar, as now pursued, wholly fails to accomplish its object. It fails also, not because too little, but because too much, is attempted. The theory of a science is taught, and the practice of a thing is neglected.

"I would respectfully urge that a new system ought to be adopted to secure a better instruction. More time - a great deal more time during, at any rate, the last year of the grammar school course - should be directed to that practice which alone enables any one to put his thoughts on paper, either correctly or legibly.... the best instruction...is apt to be that which is least pretentious. Half of the labor now expended in mastering abstract rules would produce accomplished penmen; and any child who can talk can, if the pen is familiar to his hand, with but little practice, learn to write what he thinks..."

That last comment certainly has Parker overtones. Parker was famous for having said, more or less, that he wanted children to "talk with their pencils." It should be noted that Adams, who was himself no authority on language, was diametrically opposed in his opinion on grammar to one of the greatest authorities on language who has ever lived, Professor Mario Pei of Columbia University. As mentioned elsewhere, Pei considered the study of grammar to be indispensable. So, it is interesting to note, did the early Irish monk scholars (and presumably their lay associates) who, as outlined by Louis Holtz of France, mentioned elsewhere, produced a rash of Latin grammars in the seventh century, not too long after Latin learning had arrived in Ireland with St. Patrick in the fifth century. It was these Irish monk scholars who helped to bring learning back to England, and then with the English monks, back to the Continent in the centuries that followed. Would these Irish and English monks before the tenth century have been such missionary scholars if they had not also been such grammarians?

It is not unreasonable to assume that Agassiz' belief that language in schools largely took the place of thought may have also affected his ex-pupil, William James that same academic year, 1870-1871. If the idea was familiar to audiences attending Agassiz' public lectures that year, certainly James must have known of it.

His relationship with Agassiz was hardly casual. In James' comments at the reception of The American Society of Naturalists December 30, 1896, which comments were printed in Cambridge in 1897, as Louis Agassiz: Words Spoken by Professor William James," the following is recorded on page 8:

"I had the privilege of admission to his society during the Thayer expedition to Brazil. I well remember at night, as we all swung in our hammocks in the fairy-like moonlight, on the deck of the steamer that throbbed its way up the Amazon between the forests guarding the stream on either side, how he turned and whispered, "James, are you awake?" and continued, "I cannot sleep; I am too happy; I keep thinking of these glorious plans." The plans contemplated following the Amazon to its head-waters, and penetrating the Andes in Peru....

"There is probably no public school teacher now in New England who will not tell you how Agassiz used to lock a student up in a room full of turtle shells, or lobster shells, or oyster shells, without a book or word to help him, and not let him out till he had discovered all the truths which

71

the objects contained. Some found the truths after weeks and months of lonely sorrow; others never found them."

In the three empty years in James' life, it seems possible he may have "acted" to improve reading with the sentence method, a kind of simplified version of his "stream of consciousness" ideas. After all, the sentence method concentrated on the teaching of "meaning," instead of the presumed meaninglessness of Leigh phonics, and should have been justified by the ideas of Agassiz. Interestingly enough, the "sentence method" is the variety of the "sight-word" method that Parker used at Quincy starting in 1875, six years before Farnham's book on the method appeared in print, but only two years after Farnham wrote his NEA paper. When Edwin Austin Sheldon of the Oswego, New York, State Normal and Training School published his insufficiently phonic readers in 1875, he specifically mentioned the sentence method (but considered it to be only a variation on the dominant whole-word method). (His co-author was E. Hubbard Barlow, Professor of Rhetoric and Elocution at Lafayette College, Easton, Pennsylvania, where J. M. Cattell's father was President and from which school Cattell graduated in 1880.) Obviously, by 1875, the sentence method was very, very well known. Yet no one had ever heard of the sentence method before 1870!

William James was almost certainly acquainted with the three Adams' brothers who were involved in the Quincy schools: Charles Francis Adams, Jr., John Quincy Adams, and Brooks Adams, all direct descendants of President John Adams and President John Quincy Adams. As already mentioned, one of young William James' close personal friends in Boston was young Oliver Wendell Holmes, Jr., and a fourth Adams' brother, Henry Adams, was on the staff of Harvard, when William James began teaching there in 1872, and Henry Adams was also a personal friend of William James' brother, the novelist, Henry James, by 1870. That was the Boston/Cambridge social circle in which James moved in the 1870's and it must have included all of the Adams brothers.

William James was married on July 10, 1878, to Alice Howe Gibbons, a teacher in Miss Sanger's School for Girls in Boston. On page 17 of The Death and Letters of Alice James, Ruth Bernard Yeazell's book about James' sister, Yeazell wrote:

"In May of 1878, (William James') future wife put an end to an uneasy courtship of several years by accepting his proposal of marriage."

During the time of his courtship of a schoolteacher, James must have listened to a lot of conversations on school matters besides reading the public relations releases in the newspapers which were bringing people from as far away as Syracuse, New York, to visit the Quincy, Massachusetts, schools in April, 1878, only a month before James became engaged to a Boston schoolteacher.

Although James did not complete his Principles of Psychology until 1890, he had contracted with Holt and Company to write it in June, 1878, a month after his engagement in 1878 (according to Yeazell). Therefore, James' ideas about language expressed in his 1890 text may well have been conceived by him in 1878 or before. It is impossible to assume that James was unaware in 1878 of the nearby Quincy experiment. It seems likely from James' later written comments on language in his psychology text that James would have agreed with Colonel Parker in 1878 concerning Parker's ideas on teaching beginning reading by "meaning."

Yet Parker only came to the Boston schools in 1880, and the sight-word and sentence "meaning" approach was adopted in the Boston schools at the end of the 1877-1878 school year, for use the following September, 1878. Parker was therefore not personally responsible for the initial move in Boston from "sound" to "meaning."

Philbrick, who had supported Leigh phonics, was fired as of March 1, 1878, being replaced by Samuel Eliot as Superintendent of the Boston schools. Whether Samuel Eliot was related to President Charles W. Eliot of Harvard, who lived directly across the street from the James' family on Quincy Street in Cambridge in the 1870's, is not known. (Leon Edel's Henry James: The Conquest of London - 1870-1881, page 20, recorded that Eliot's home was opposite the James' family home.) What is evident from the quality of Philbrick's reports compared to Samuel Eliot's reports, however, is that the highly intelligent and competent Philbrick was replaced by an academic hack.

So, two years before Parker arrived, the sight-word method had already been moved into the Boston schools, displacing the phonic Leigh print which had been so successful before Philbrick was fired. Therefore, Philbricks' Leigh phonics obviously had determined enemies long before Parker showed up on the Boston scene. It must have been they who hired Parker in 1880! As the School Committee said in the Annual Report of the School Committee of the City of Boston - 1871, pages 7 to 9, in telling of the great success of the Leigh phonics method, before it had spread into almost all the Boston schools through the voluntary choice of the schools themselves:

"When the system of Dr. Leigh is mentioned, many excellent people, committee men, teachers and parents, shake their heads incredulously. It has been stigmatized as a 'fancy method.' Philosophers have proved (to their own satisfaction) that the plan is vicious. Practical men (who have never examined it) declare that its results are barren. Teachers (averse to change) say they have no difficulty now; that the old way is good enough for them.

"We beg leave to say that six years of careful experiment in several schools in this city have shown the best results from this system... Within six months ordinary pupils under this system get nearly through the second reader, - a point which pupils by the old method are always eighteen months, and often two years in reaching. This is a constant, unvarying result.... At an exhibition of a primary class in the Lincoln District, several pupils who had been less than eighteen months under instruction read at sight from books they had never seen."

But the facts in the report for 1870-1871 on the success of Leigh phonics did not move Philbrick's opponents, including, very interestingly, the "philosophers," who "have proved (to their own satisfaction) that the plan is vicious." It was only a year before the School Committee's 1871 comment about "philosophers" that Henry James spoke of his brother's metaphysical club, in which they argued humorlessly and never left the topic. Was William James one of the "philosophers" disapproving of Leigh phonics?

Rudolph R. Reeder (1859-?), who in 1900 was Instructor in Theory and Practice of Teaching, Teachers College, Columbia University, wrote The Historical Development of School Readers and of Method in Teaching Reading, Columbia University Contributions to Philosophy, Psychology and Education, Volume 8. No. 2, The Macmillan Company, New York, May, 1900. Bound immediately after it in the same volume, but dated 1901, appeared Vol. 8, Nos. 3-4. Notes on Child Study, by Edward Lee Thorndike, Adjunct Professor of Psychology, Teachers College, Columbia University. Reeder and Thorndike must have been well acquainted with one another, and since Thorndike was so closely associated with Cattell of Columbia University, it seems likely Reeder would have also been an associate of Cattell.

It is highly interesting that Reeder, writing in 1900, knew enough to check Philbrick's annual report from Boston 28 years before in 1872 (page 77) when Reeder himself was only thirteen years old. Reeder quoted Philbrick's strong plea for the spelling book and Philbrick's comment that the spelling book's antagonist was "the modern educational maxim, ideas before words." The Boston annual reports each year were encyclopedic, yet Reeder could put his finger on a specific pertinent quotation from one 28 years before, even though he apparently had no personal connection with Boston. Reeder said that Philbrick had stated further that "Reading is spelling on the book, naming the letters, and syllabicating." Yet poor Philbrick was fired in 1878, 22 years before Reeder wrote, and "spelling on the book, naming the letters, and syllabicating" were not only thrown out of Boston with Philbrick but were largely forgotten along with Philbrick himself.

It is unlikely that Reeder could have known Philbrick, who died about 1885 and whose name dropped into oblivion. It is probable that Reeder was directed to Philbrick's comments buried deeply in the many annual volumes of the encyclopedic Boston schools' reports by someone else. That would have been someone who knew there had been a conflict in Boston back in 1878, and who could isolate specific items from the encyclopedic Boston school reports back to 1872 (which indicates, interestingly, a period of conflict running from at least 1872 to 1878).

That person might have been Cattell, who was then at Columbia University as was Reeder, and who could have learned of Philbrick's comments through his close friend, William James, or possibly through his teacher at Lafayette College, Professor Francis A. March. It is highly improbable that Cattell could have found Philbrick's comments by himself, as Cattell was only twelve years old in 1872 and was living in Pennsylvania, while his close friend in later years, William James, was thirty years old in 1872 and living in Cambridge, right across the Charles River from Philbrick's Boston. In 1872, James had just begun teaching at Harvard, across the river from Boston. James' former professor and close associate, Agassiz, was also still teaching at Harvard, and Agassiz had been campaigning against empty language at least from the 1870-1871 academic year. The neighbor who lived across the street from the James' family home in Cambridge, President Eliot of Harvard, had possibly already begun his campaign for real literature in school readers by 1869, to judge from his collected writings mentioned previously.

The founding of the "Board of Supervisors" operating under the Boston School Committee, of which board Parker eventually became a member, dated from the school year 1877-1878, and presumably only from March 1, 1878, the date Philbrick was fired. The board filed its "sixth annual report of their work as a Board and as Supervisors, for the school year beginning Sept. 1, 1882," on September 25, 1883, which supports the presumed date of their organization as March 1, 1878. They were obviously a very busy group in 1882-83, as they said in their 1883 report they had held seventy-four meetings in the year from September 1, 1882 to September 1, 1883. According to this report, their duties were "specified in the Rules and Regulations of the School Committee under Sections 136-153 inclusive," which it would be of interest to see. This 1883 report of the board referred to its 1883 paper on reading, which has been discussed, and said further, under "Reading:"

"No subject has attracted more attention among the teachers of the country than 'Reading' as taught in the public schools. No one subject comprehends so much nor is so far-reaching in its effects upon the training of the child.

"During the present year the Board of Supervisors, at the request of the School Committee, undertook to revise the whole plan of teaching reading in the Primary Schools, and, if possible, to present some method that might be adopted, and followed by all the Primary teachers of the city.

"In the plan presented (School Document No. 1, 1883) the pupil begins by learning a few familiar words as names of objects equally familiar. A few other common words are also learned, that short sentences may be formed and written on the black-board. These sentences are carefully copied by the children upon their slates, more to impress the form of the word or the sentence upon the child's mind, than because of its value as an exercise in writing.

"Constant effort is made to associate the spoken or written word with the idea it is intended to convey.

"Very soon the pupil's attention is called to the sounds of the letters, uttering them only in imitation of the teacher, that the ear of the pupil may be carefully trained from the first to recognize correct sounds."

Note the clear admission here that "phonics" at this beginning stage was concerned only with pronunciation and had nothing to do with decoding.

"When so much has been accomplished the progress becomes exceedingly rapid. Each new word learned is a help to the learning of analogous words, and the skill of the teacher is shown in the selection of such new words as will present the fewest difficulties to the pupil.

"A large number of words has been arranged in classes, and printed in a convenient form in the school document referred to for the purpose of assisting the teacher in her selection, and facilitating her work in its earliest stages."

Note the clear endorsement of two-step phony phonics: the comparing of one whole meaning-bearing word to other whole sight words.

"It is confidently believed by the Board of Supervisors that when the plan is thoroughly understood, and skillfully carried out in all its details by the Primary teachers, excellent results will be gained.

"Individual preferences as to methods must give way to the general good, and if the best, as we conceive it, cannot be had, the best that we can have, ought to be accepted in good faith.

"This document has been issued by the authority of the School Board; and a copy has been placed in the hands of each Primary teacher as a guide in this department of her work in the future."

This so-reasonable-sounding document is a cushioned announcement that any primary-grades teacher who used "sound" to teach beginning reading could anticipate being fired. It was the underpaid and overworked women teachers with enormous primary grade classes in Boston who had been doing the real work of teaching. They had, almost without exception, been using Leigh phonics successfully for some years before 1878, since almost every school district in Boston had freely chosen to use Leigh phonics. Yet after five years of "change," by 1883, the controlling vise of the change-agents had tightened: if first-grade teachers in 1883 did not drop the Leigh phonics they had used so successfully and teach sight-words in its place, they could anticipate being fired.

Most meaningfully, portions of the unsigned 1883 paper, Method of Teaching Reading in the Primary Schools, published by the Board of Supervisors for the Public Schools of Boston in 1883, sound exactly like James' prose and certainly contain his ideas about "meaning" and sentences. Furthermore, the portions could only have been written by someone trained in psychology, in the modern sense. It is my opinion that they were written by James sometime before 1882, at which time he left Harvard on a year's leave of absence.

Concerning the only other probable authors, Colonel Parker had absorbed a lot of Hegelian ideas in Germany from 1872 to 1874 but had not studied with the psychologist Wundt. The psychologist G. Stanley Hall by 1883 was in Baltimore training the future psychologists Cattell and Dewey at Johns Hopkins. Josiah Royce had studied logic briefly with Wundt and practical philosophy and metaphysics with Lotze in Germany, and, it is true, formed a Psychology Club at the University of

California in 1880, but a dominant influence on Royce was from William James, whose friend he had become when James gave lectures at Johns Hopkins University in 1878. By September, 1882, Royce had left the University of California to fill in for James while James was on sabbatical leave in the academic year of 1882-1883 Royce stayed permanently at Harvard and remained a close friend of James, but Royce was primarily a philosopher. (Biographical data is contained in The Letters of Josiah Royce, Edited and with an Introduction by John Clendenning. The University of Chicago Press. Chicago: 1970.) Royce would hardly have become involved in writing a tract for the Boston public schools immediately upon becoming a substitute instructor at Harvard in the academic year 1882-1883. That left William James as the only psychologist, in the modern sense, other than Hall and George Trumbull Ladd (1842-1921), anywhere in America before 1883.

# Appendix 3

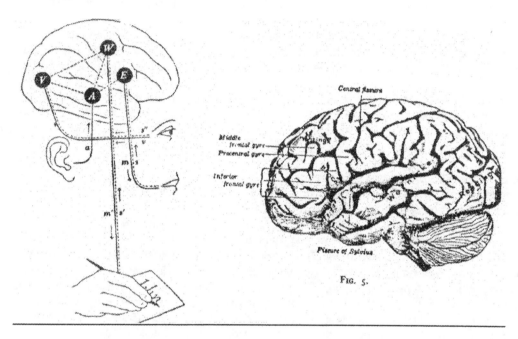

FIG. 5.

---

## Concerning the Different and Opposite Conditioned Reflexes in Reading, and Their Brain-Based Origin

Reference has been made in this book to the fact that work done on stroke patients had revealed, long before William James wrote his 1890 Principles of Psychology, that sound-bearing print is processed through the left angular gyrus area in the back of the brain.

On page 37, in his Figure 18, James reproduced an illustration from an 1887 book, Aphasia, by James Ross, which clearly showed the areas in the brain, including the angular gyrus area, which are used sequentially in reading (and writing). The illustration is reproduced above. On the diagram, "A" marked Wernicke's area ("auditory"), "E" marked Broca's area ("expressive"), "W" marked writing, and "V" marked the angular gyrus area ("visual").

James also included on page 25, in his Figure 11, a diagram of the brain with clear labels on the areas known as Broca's and Wernicke's, and on page 36, in his Figure 17, a diagram of the brain which showed the "Angular Conv." (obviously, the angular gyrus area).

Those areas also appeared in a diagram of the brain in the 1911 text, Elements of Physiological Psychology, by Ladd and Woodworth. For purposes of illustration, that diagram (labeled Fig. 5. in that text) is also reproduced above.

Summarizing much work that had been done in Europe, William James reported at length on language in his 1890 book, The Principles of Psychology. On pages 25, 26, 32,33, 35, 36 and 37, James referred to Broca's area, first identified by Broca in 1861. Broca's area is on the lower front lobe of the surface layer of the brain's cortex and is normally in the left hemisphere. James called the aphasia resulting from damage to Broca's area "motor aphasia." Those patients might understand speech but not be able to produce it. It seems apparent that Broca's area deals with the production of syllable sounds.

James also reported in 1890 on the effect of damage to Wernicke's area, producing what he called "sensory aphasia" (pages 35, 36, 37). In sensory aphasia, aphasics do not understand the meaning of words, even though they can hear them. James said (page 35):

> "Wernicke was the first to discriminate those cases in which the patient can not even understand speech from those in which he can understand, only not talk; and to ascribe the former condition to lesion of the temporal lobe. The condition in question is word-deafness...."

Broca's area must process syllable sounds, but Wernicke's area must process word meanings.

The literature indicates that spoken word meanings are handled through the front of Wernicke's area, and printed word meanings through the back, in the angular gyrus region. (The angular gyrus is now considered part of Wernicke's area, although it was considered to be separate from it in James' day).

It appears self-evident that spoken language has three levels, the first two of which are processed automatically: the syllable level (presumably processed through Broca's area) and the syntax/word level (presumably processed through Wernicke's area). The final level, "meaning," is conscious and is handled in the front of the brain.

At the syntax/word level, it is postulated that it is syntax which generates the words, and not the other way around. Words are, after all, only parts of speech - which is to say, parts of syntax. William H. Calvin, Ph. D., and George A. Ojemann, M. D., in their book, Inside the Brain, A Mentor Book, New York, 1980, reported that they found that grammar (syntax) occupied a different site from word meanings in Wernicke's area on the cortex, which appears to support this assumption. Furthermore, Sid J. Segalowitz, in his book, Two Sides of the Brain, Prentice-Hall, Inc., Englewood Cliffs, New Jersey, 1983, reported that some aphasic patients, who were incapable of understanding the meaning of speech but who retained the ability to repeat other people's speech, have been found to correct grammar in repeating heard sentences. Obviously, syntax was controlling their production of words, and it was doing so at the automatic, not conscious, level since those patients were incapable of understanding word meanings. That indicates that the automatic production of "syntax" precedes and generates "words."

William James reported on an elaborate study by Naunyn on 71 cases of aphasia (Nothnagel and Naunyn, Die Localization in den Gehirnkrankheiten, Wiesbaden, 1887), and quoted other authors on the subject. (It is surprising to find aphasia mentioned so seldom in the literature since then.) James said in 1890 (p. 37):

> "Naunyn... plotting out on a diagram of the hemisphere the 71 irreproachable reported cases of aphasia which he was able to collect, finds that the lesions concentrate themselves in three places: first, on Broca's centre; second, on Wernicke's; third on the supramarginal and angular gyri under which those fibres pass which connect the visual centre with the rest of the brain..."

Dr. Wilder Penfield in his book, The Mystery of the Mind, Princeton University Press, Princeton, New Jersey: 1975, and Dr. Calvin and Dr. Ojemann in their book publish illustrations which include James' third section described above (the angular gyrus area) as part of Wernicke's area, rather than showing it separately. The Encyclopedia Britannica illustration of the brain, page 76, Volume 4 (1963), shows the same site for the left angular gyrus, although it is not specifically labeled as part of Wernicke's area.

Calvin and Ojemann referred to a patient who had lost his reading ability, but only that portion, apparently, which was sound-bearing. They then included a drawing of the brain showing where a computerized tomographic scan had revealed the location of that patient's stroke. It was clearly in the same area as that labeled the angular gyrus area in the illustrations mentioned above.

Dr. Hilde L. Mosse wrote (page 52, The Complete Handbook of Reading Disorders, Human Sciences Press, Inc., New York, 1982):

"The brain does not operate in isolated units but this does not mean that we cannot pin-point anatomically specific areas in the brain that have very specialized functions... damage to certain crucial shunts or sidings invariably causes loss of function. Brodmann's area 39 in the angular gyrus in the parietal lobes, which is located at the center of the reading region, is such a shunt. Any kind of damage to it causes Alexia (complete inability to read), and at least a partial Agraphia (an inability to write). This does not mean that the neurophysiologic basis for reading is located in area 39 exclusively. This area is only one part, even though a crucial one, of the entire cerebral reading apparatus."

Dr. Mosse referred (page 46) to Norbert Wiener, who originated the scientific method he called cybernetics, and said that others have applied communication engineering to the study of the brain. The most practical results have been in producing a machine to read to the blind, the Kurzweil Reading Machine. Mosse said (p. 46-47)

"The Kurzweil Reading Machine consists of an optical scanner on which printed material is placed, a computer, and a small control unit with 30 buttons. A (small) program tape is inserted.... The scanner searches the page, finds the top line, and moves across the text, line by line. It takes an electronic picture of each word, which the computer analyzes into letters. The letters are then blended according to phonetic rules into spoken words....

"Wiener and McCulloch suggested that the brain might also use a 'scanning apparatus'...."

Professor Frank Smith, the renowned psycholinguist, who promotes "meaning" in the teaching of beginning reading and opposes "sound," wrote in his book, Reading Without Nonsense:

"Skill in reading depends on using the eyes as little as possible (p.9.)

"If you are not making errors when you read, you are probably not reading efficiently. (p.33.)

"The reason phonics does not work for children or for computers is that the links between the letters and sounds cannot be specified.... They are too complex. (p. 51-52.)"

As Dr. Rudolph Flesch pointed out in his 1981 book, Why Johnny STILL Can't Read (p. 27), concerning Smith's last statement:

"This would be a splendid argument against phonics except for the awkward fact [of the] Kurzweil Reading Machine."

# Appendix 4

Concerning the Exercise of Influence, ibid, pages 1612-1615

### CONCERNING INFLUENCE

Excerpts from pages 1612-1615, Volume III
The History of Beginning Reading, From Teaching by
Sound to Teaching by Meaning
By Geraldine E. Rodgers, 2001, 1st Books Library

It is also of interest that The Cumulative Book Index, 1928-1932 indicated that the American Library Association was publishing material concerning primers and readers. At the end of the "Primer" section, under "Bibliography," appeared:

"American library association. Section for library work with children. Committee on readers and primers. Readers and primers. pa per 10 45c '29 A.L.A."

This general material, with dates of 1931 and 1933, was listed in the card catalog of the Library of Congress, and has been listed at the beginning of this bibliography, but was not available when I requested it at the Library of Congress.

The Cattell manuscript files at the Library of Congress have two interesting typed sheets, on which the name of the American Library Association appeared. Cattell was a superb organizer (which William James acknowledged in one of his letters to Cattell, now in the Library of Congress manuscript files). These two typed pages are reproduced on the following two pages, and might be seen as kinds of organization charts. The many American associations, like the American Library Association, which were listed on each sheet reached into almost every area of American cultural life. Each had a suggested representative named for the two proposed new master organizations to be concerned with "education." At the bottom of each list appeared the American Association for the Advancement of Science, to be represented by Cattell who at that time was the Chairman of its Executive Committee, a post which he held for many years.

If the two proposed organizations on the two copies reproduced on the following pages, or any organizations like them, ever materialized, with their named representatives chosen by the arch-activist Cattell, they operated safely outside the public sphere and could exert massive influence from the top to reach all of America, insulated from voters at the polls.

The Constitution authorized the United States Congress and the office of the Presidency to set public policy and to steer the course of this nation. Therefore, for such unauthorized privately organized groups quietly to take over the functions of the elected Congress and the elected Presidency can best be described as sedition. Such activity in 1917 by men with apparent ties to Cattell and his associates had raised a furor in Congress, which unfortunately died down because of the advent of World War I. (See Lance J. Klass's book, The Leipzig Connection, with Paolo Lionni.)

The United States of America has needed laws for a very long time which can serve at least to publicize such sub-rosa quasi-legal seditious activities. After all, no one and no group has any "right" to control other people and the environment of other people without publicly announcing their intentions to do so. After all, that is the purpose for the legal listings in newspapers of tax sales on properties with back taxes, and for public notices on similar things. Whether Cattell's proposed organizations ever existed as suggested on his typed sheets is not known. At the very least, such activities should have been announced ahead of time publicly, and any meetings of such a group should always have been open to the public. However, that such was the intent is very doubtful. Yet those two typed sheets do demonstrate how effectively illicit influence can, potentially, be exercised on the life of this entire nation, and how it is probably being exercised, without the properly informed consent of the voting public, at this very time.

*(Reproduced from the Cattell Manuscript Files, Library of Congress, Washington, DC)*

It seems very possible that the above ALA "Committee on readers and primers" was influenced by Cattell and his clique of "experts" through some such net of influence as outlined on the reproductions just shown. Certainly uncontrolled vocabulary library books for children posed a real stumbling block to the anticipated arrival of the deaf-mute-method readers, with their appallingly impoverished vocabulary.

Library books for children would have had to change in tandem with school books, and they did change, it should be remarked. Controlled vocabulary took over most of children's literature some time after 1929. Presumably many of the great number of isolated titles appearing under "Readers" in The Cumulative Book Index, 1928-1932 were such controlled vocabulary "story" books. They probably found their way into American libraries as alternatives for unadapted copies of such uncontrolled vocabulary works as Tom Sawyer, Pinnochio, Winnie the Pooh and Alice in Wonderland. When the controlled-vocabulary library books finally arrived some time after 1929 to function as replacements for real children's literature, the attack on American literacy had begun in earnest.

***************

# Appendix 5

Concerning the Effects of Word Frequencies, ibid, pages 9-10

Concerning the Effect of Word Frequencies,
from pages 9-10.
Volume I, The History of Beginning Reading, by
Geraldine E. Rodgers, 4/13/01, 1st Books Library

That word is truly representative of most of the words in the English language, the vast majority of which do not appear at all in Thorndike's count. Yet they appear with frequencies that are very high in certain areas of discussion. Teachers were counseled to "teach" words at the lower frequencies in Thorndike's text depending on their "importance." Yet how could any teacher possibly evaluate the ultimate "importance" of a particular word for a particular child? Why not let the child sound out ALL the words he encounters in print and acquire their meaning in print just as he does in conversation: by its context or by the dictionary?

As has been mentioned, in A Measurement of Ability in Spelling in 1915, Ayres referred to the fascinating fact that only about fifty high-frequency words account for about half of any written context. (The Ladybird material assumed that 100 words accounted for half, but whether the number is fifty or a hundred, it is still extremely small.) That general fact surely had to be known by Thorndike, and yet he made no reference to it. Yet the peculiar patterns formed by word-frequencies can become obvious by extrapolating from some of the word frequency figures that Thorndike did give for words above the two thousand most common. (He obscured facts on the two thousand most common.) However, unless someone knew ahead of time that word frequencies produce such peculiar patterns, it is highly unlikely that it would occur to him to dig out those patterns from Thorndike's frequency figures.

On page x of The Teacher's Word Book of 30,000 Words, Thorndike said that 1,069 AA words occurred 100 times or more in every million words. The most meaningful word in that description was "more," since it is evident from Ayres' and others' work that only 50 or 100 of those 1,069 words would have accounted for one half, or 500,000, of those million running words, and the entire 1,069 would have accounted for about nine-tenths, or 900,000 of those running words. Yet Thorndike did not even hint at such extremely interesting and peculiar facts.

Also on page x appeared the fact that the 952 words labeled "A" had appeared between 50 to 99 times per million. However, after the vague statistics for the 1,069 and 952 most common words, clear statistics finally appeared, because these statements were followed by a table for the number of words occurring between 49 times per million and one per million. After each entry, such as 49 times per million, appeared the number of words with that frequency. The table began with listing the number 36 for the 36 words which had appeared 49 times, and ended with 5,209, for the 5,209 words which had apeared only once in a million running words. What is most notable is the great increase of numbers of words, as the numbers of times that words occur greatly decrease. To illustrate, the first four and the last four entries were as follows:

| Number of Occurrences Per Million Words | Number of Words At That Frequency |
|---|---|
| 49 | 36 |
| 48 | 35 |
| 47 | 33 |
| 46 | 38 |
| ..... | ..... |
| 4 | 1,064 |
| 3 | 1,442 |
| 2 | 2,503 |
| 1 | 5,209 |

Those last four entries total 10,218 words out of Thorndike's first 20,000, or more than half. Yet, as a percentage of the running million words, they account for only 1.9 per cent of the total. A study based on the far simpler material of letters, referred to previously, found that only three thousand of the highest

85

frequency words accounted for all but about two percent of that simpler material. However, since Thorndike's words were selected from the far heavier content of real literature, it is not surprising that about 9,000 plus words accounted for 98% of that heavier material, although only 3,000 words accounted for 98% of the far simpler material.

Thorndike had extended the 20,000 word list of 1931 to 30,000 words in this 1944 revision prepared with Irving Lorge, published by Teachers College Press, Teachers College, Columbia University, New York. Explaining the additional 10,000 words over the 20,000 of 1931, Thorndike stated on page x that 9,202 words had occurred less than once a million, but oftener than four times in 18 million words. That works out to between 0.2 per cent to 0.9 percent of each million words. For the sake of argument, those words might be said to occupy no more than 0.6 percent of the total million (and probably considerably less). A further 1,358 words were listed that occurred four times in 18 million words, bringing the 1944 total to 30,000 words. Those last 1,358 words would occupy .03 percent of a million words.

Therefore, Thorndike's "literature" words from about 10,000 to about 20,000 frequency would occupy 1.9 per cent of a running selection; and the words from 20,000 to 30,000 would occupy the total of about 0.6 per cent and 0.03 percent, or about 0.63 percent. The grand total of all the words from 10,000 to 30,000 would amount to only about 2.53 per cent of any page of print. (What is most surprising about the entries from 20,000 to 30,000 is the fact that such great numbers of them are not at all unusual, but are very ordinary, well known words. Therefore, by extrapolation, so must many words above the 30,000-word-level be familiar to most people.) Yet Thorndike had sampled only 30,000 words, and an unabridged dictionary has about half a million words. It is obvious that most of the words in that dictionary, if not already listed by Thorndike, must occur somewhere at the frequency level of one or two per cent, or less, of any selection.

Despite their very infrequent use, would anyone be so mad as to assume we could function as a society without the use of those hundreds of thousands of low-frequency words, none of which appeared on the Thorndike count? Why then, should not children be taught to read all such words by themselves, and be drilled in the use of a dictionary when the context does not provide sufficient help in figuring out meanings?

Thorndike's first tabulation in 1921 covered 10,000 words, and his final tabulation some twenty years later covered 30,000 words. Yet Thorndike's method of grouping words totally obscured that fascinating fact about word frequencies: the higher the frequency of a word, the greater is the percentage of a person's total spoken and written vocabulary that it occupies, and the lower the frequency of a word, the smaller is the percentage of an individual's total spoken and written vocabulary that it occupies. Count the number of times the word "the" is used in the preceding sentence, for example, in contrast to the word "fascinating."

Most of an educated person's vocabulary of the rarer words is learned through reading. Yet the deaf-mute reading method has resulted in rigid control of the vocabulary in children's books so that children's vocabulary cannot grow normally through exposure to books. In addition, the deaf-mute method also cripples children's decoding skills so that they will never be able to read with ease any materials which have normal, uncontrolled vocabularies. As a result, children's vocabularies do not greatly increase even when they are exposed to pre-1930 uncontrolled-vocabulary children's books or any adult materials which have uncontrolled vocabularies.

Children taught by the "meaning" method are crippled in their vocabulary development in the same way that a badly taught deaf-mute is crippled. They quite literally cannot easily "hear" new words when they are reading. Such artificially-deafened children never reach, and many never even remotely approach, the adult vocabulary level of which they had been potentially capable.

Printed in the United States
by Baker & Taylor Publisher Services